SUBMARINES

OF WORLD WAR II

SUBMARINES
OF WORLD WAR II

John Ward

MBI Publishing Company

This edition first published in 2001 by MBI Publishing
Company, Galtier Plaza, Suite 200
380 Jackson Street, St. Paul, MN 55101-3885 USA

The information in this book is true and complete to the best
of our knowledge. All recommendations are made without any
guarantee on the part of the author or publisher, who also
disclaim any liability incurred in connection with the use of this
data or specified details.

We recognize that some words, model names and
designations, for example, mentioned herein are the property
of the trademark holder. We use them for identification
purposes only. This is not an official publication.

MBI Publishing Company books are also available at discounts
in bulk quantity for industrial or sales-promotional use. For
details write to Special Sales Manager at Motorbooks
International Wholesalers & Distributors, Galtier Plaza, Suite
200, 380 Jackson Street, St. Paul, MN 55101-3885 USA

Library of Congress Cataloging-in-Publication Data Available.

ISBN 0-7603-1170-6

Printed in Hong Kong

Editorial and design
Brown Partworks Limited
8 Chapel Place
Rivington Street
London
EC2A 3DQ
UK

Editor: Anne Cree
Picture research: Antony Shaw
Design: Siobhán Gallagher
Production: Matt Weyland

Picture Credits
All photographs The Robert Hunt Library except the
following:
Novosti: 87, 89, 91, 92, 93
Popperfoto: 35, 58, 63, 68
The Submarine Museum: 6, 10, 29, 32, 34, 38,
51, 54, 55, 56, 74, 79
TRH Pictures: 7, 8, 9, 11, 12, 13, 14, 16, 17, 18,
19, 21, 22, 26, 27, 28, 30, 33, 36, 37, 39, 40,
41, 43, 44, 47, 53, 59, 60, 61, 70, 72, 73, 75,
80, 82, 85

CONTENTS

ARGONAUTE

SPECIFICATIONS

ARGONAUTE

Displacement surfaced: **640tnes (630t)**	Performance surfaced: **13.5 knots**
Displacement submerged: **811tnes (798t)**	Performance submerged: **7.5 knots**
Machinery: **two screws, diesel/electric motors; 1300/1000hp**	Armament: **six 550mm (21.7in) TT; one 75mm (3in) gun**
Length: **63.4m (208ft 11in)**	Surface range: **4260km (2300nm) at 7.5 knots**
Beam: **5.2m (17ft)**	Crew: **41**
Draught: **3.61m (11ft 9in)**	Launch date: **23 May 1929**

Rated as a second-class submarine, *Argonaute* and her four sister boats (*Arethuse, Atalante, La Sultane* and *La Vestale*) were authorized under the three successive construction programmes initiated in 1926 (two boats), 1927 (one boat) and 1929 (two boats). All five boats were built by Schneider, their design being based on the firm's earlier class of 600-tonne (590-ton) submarines.

Argonaute was laid down in April 1928 and completed some four years later in July 1932. Upon completing her trials she was assigned to the French submarine forces in the Mediterranean. *Argonaute* was based at Oran, and she was still there when France fell to Nazi Germany in June 1940.

Under the terms of the Franco–German Armistice she was handed over to the Vichy French Navy, and in November 1942 her crew actively resisted the Allied landings in North Africa, putting to sea with a few other French vessels in a futile attempt to attack the Anglo–American invasion fleet.

Argonaute and another submarine were sunk by the British warships *Achates* and *Westcott* off Oran on 8 November. One of *Argonaute*'s sister boats, *La Sultane*, subsequently served with the Allied naval forces in the Mediterranean.

CALYPSO

One of four 600-tonne (590-ton) Circe-class submarines laid down in 1923 by Schneider-Laubeuf, *Calypso* was completed in 1929. These second-class boats were well-armed and manoeuvrable, but they were cramped internally and crew conditions were poor, hence the requirement for the larger 630-tonne (620-ton) class that followed them.

In addition to the four Circe class submarines, four 600-tonne (590-ton) boats (the Sirene class) were built by A.C. de la Loire and four (the Ariane class) by A.C. Augustin-Normand. Of *Calypso*'s sister boats (some of which are shown above), the *Doris* became an early war casualty. In April 1940, while serving with the 10th Submarine Flotilla, she deployed to Harwich together with five other French submarines to reinforce the Royal Navy's boats, and on 10 May she was sunk by the German submarine *U-9* off the Dutch coast.

The other boats of the Circe class were deployed to the Mediterranean. *Thetis* was scuttled at Toulon on 27 November 1942 just before German forces occupied the port, while *Circe* and *Calypso* were seized by the enemy at Bizerta, Tunisia, on 8 December. *Circe* was allocated to the Italian Navy and was scuttled in May 1943, while *Calypso* was destroyed in an air attack on 30 January of that year.

SPECIFICATIONS

CALYPSO

Displacement surfaced: **625tnes (615t)**	*Performance surfaced:* **14 knots**
Displacement submerged: **788tnes (776t)**	*Performance submerged:* **7.5 knots**
Machinery: **two screws, diesel- electric motors, 1250/1000hpp**	*Armament:* **seven 550mm (21.7in) TT; one 75mm (3in) gun**
Length: **62.48m (205ft)**	*Surface range:* **6482km (3500nm) at 10 knots**
Beam: **5.40m (17ft 9in)**	*Crew:* **41**
Draught: **3.90m (12ft 9in)**	*Launch date:* **15 January 1926**

CASABIANCA

SPECIFICATIONS

CASABIANCA

Displacement surfaced: **1595tnes (1570t)**	**Performance surfaced:** **17–20 knots**
Displacement submerged: **2117tnes (2084t)**	**Performance submerged:** **10 knots**
Machinery: **twin screws, diesel/electric motors; 2900/1800hp**	**Armament:** **nine 550mm (21.7in) and two 400mm (15.7in) TT; one 100mm (3.9in) gun**
Length: **92.3m (210ft)**	**Surface range:** **18,530km (10,000nm) at 10 knots**
Beam: **8.2m (18ft 7in)**	**Crew:** **61**
Draught: **4.7m (10ft 9in)**	**Launch date:** **2 February 1935**

Laid down in 1931, *Casabianca* was an ocean-going submarine of the Redoutable class. These first-class submarines, of which there were 29 in total, were double-hulled boats with excellent handling qualities and a good turn of speed on the surface.

The major drawback of Redoutable-class submarines was that it took them up to 50 seconds to dive, which was thought to be rather slow at a time when anti-submarine aircraft were presenting an increasing threat at sea.

The Redoutable-class was not without its misfortunes, either. One of the first series boats, *Promethee*, sank during a trials exercise on 8 July 1942, and another, *Phenix*, disappeared without trace off French Indo-China on 15 June 1939. Seven boats were scuttled at Toulon in November 1942 when German forces occupied the south of France, four were scuttled at Brest, and others were lost in Allied air attacks on French colonial territory. One boat, *Protee*, was probably lost in a German depth-charge attack, while *Sfax* was torpedoed in error by the German submarine *U-37* after France had surrendered.

Casabianca, along with the Free French Forces, played a major part in the liberation of Corsica, sinking a German patrol craft and damaging another.

ESPADON

The Requin ("Shark") class of nine ocean-going submarines, to which *Espadon* ("Swordfish") belonged, were the first of their type to be designed in France after World War I, and their technology incorporated a great deal gleaned from the study of captured German U-boats in that conflict.

The Requin class carried a heavy offensive armament, with four bow, two stern and two twin torpedo tubes mounted in containers in the casing. These could be remotely trained either submerged or on the surface, but could not be reloaded at sea. The boats were double-hulled and had a diving depth of 80m (250ft). All the Requin class boats were fully refitted and modernized between 1935 and 1937.

Eight of the group were lost during World War II. On 8 December 1942, *Espadon* was one of four boats captured by the Italians at Bizerta; she was subsequently commissioned by the Italian Navy as the *FR114*, and on 13 September 1943 she was scuttled by the Germans at Castellammare di Stabia while being converted as a transport submarine.

The same fate was to befall two of *Espadon*'s sisters, *Requin* and *Dauphin*. Another boat, *Phoque*, became operational with the Italian Navy and was sunk in an air attack.

SPECIFICATIONS

ESPADON

Displacement surfaced: **1168tnes (1150t)**	Performance surfaced: **15 knots**
Displacement submerged: **1464tnes (1441t)**	Performance submerged: **9 knots**
Machinery: **twin screws, diesel/electric motors; 2900/1800hp**	Armament: **10 533mm (21in) TT; one 100mm (3.9in) gun**
Length: **78.2m (256ft 9in)**	Surface range: **10,469km (5650nm) at 10 knots**
Beam: **6.8m (22ft 5in)**	Crew: **54**
Draught: **5m (16ft 9in)**	Launch date: **28 May 1926**

JUNON

SPECIFICATIONS

JUNON

Displacement surfaced: **672tnes (662t)**	Performance surfaced: **15 knots**
Displacement submerged: **869tnes (856t)**	Performance submerged: **9.3 knots**
Machinery: **two screws, diesel/electric motors; 1800/1230hp**	Armament: **six 550mm (21.7in) and three 400mm (15.7in) TT; one 75mm (3in) gun**
Length: **68.10m (223ft 5in)**	Surface range: **7400km (4000nm) at 10 knots**
Beam: **5.62m (18ft 5in)**	Crew: **42**
Draught: **4.03m (13ft 3in)**	Launch date: **15 September 1935**

Authorized in 1930, the Minerve class of six submarines, *Junon* being one of them, represented a determined attempt by the French Admiralty to standardize the design of the earlier 630-tonne (620-ton) types, which had many variations despite being produced to the same specification.

Before the French collapse in 1940, *Junon* and *Minerve* managed to escape across the English Channel to Plymouth. *Minerve* had in fact been fully stripped down by the French at Cherbourg when the Germans broke through at Sedan on 19 May 1940; it was only after an epic effort by French engineers that she was made ready for sea just before the enemy arrived at the port.

Both boats subsequently served with distinction with the Free French Naval Forces, carrying out numerous war patrols in the Norwegian Sea and the Arctic. *Junon*'s commander was Lt Querville.

The boat survived the war and was sold for scrap in 1954; *Minerve* was wrecked in September 1945. The other three Minerve-class boats, *Venus*, *Ceres* and *Pallas* were all scuttled in 1942, the last two at Oran, where they were later refloated and scrapped; and *Iris* sailed for Barcelona, where she was interned until the end of the war. She was broken up in 1954.

MINERVE

After her escape from Cherbourg and arrival at Plymouth (see entry for *Junon* on the previous page), *Minerve*, under the command of Lt Sonneville, joined the Scottish-based 9th Submarine Flotilla, which also included the RN submarine *Sealion* and the Dutch boats *O21* and *O23*.

Minerve's operations off the Norwegian coast began in February 1941, and on 19 April that same year, while engaged in attacking an enemy convoy, she was heavily depth-charged by German escorts and narrowly escaped being sunk.

In May 1941 *Minerve* took part in the hunt for the German battleship *Bismarck* and the heavy cruiser *Prinz Eugen*, which were attempting to break out into the North Atlantic. Together with the RN submarine *Uproar (P31)* she was sent north to search for the *Bismarck* after the latter had refuelled in a fjord near Bergen, but neither submarine was able to locate the elusive battleship.

Later in 1941, *Minerve* operated in concert with another French submarine, *Rubis*, and in July 1942 she operated in the Arctic with eight British submarines, stationed in two lines south of Bear Island to protect the ill-fated convoy PQ.17, which was later virtually destroyed by air and U-boat attacks.

SPECIFICATIONS

MINERVE

Displacement surfaced: **672tnes (662t)**	Performance surfaced: **15 knots**
Displacement submerged: **869tnes (856t)**	Performance submerged: **9.3 knots**
Machinery: **two screws, diesel/electric motors; 1800/1230hp**	Armament: **six 550mm (21.7in) and three 400mm (15.7in) TT; one 75mm (3in) gun**
Length: **68.10m (223ft 5in)**	Surface range: **7400km (4000nm) at 10 knots**
Beam: **5.62m (18ft 5in)**	Crew: **42**
Draught: **4.03m (13ft 3in)**	Launch date: **23 October 1934**

NARVAL

SPECIFICATIONS

NARVAL

Displacement surfaced: **974tnes (990t)**	Performance surfaced: **15 knots**
Displacement submerged: **1464tnes (1441t)**	Performance submerged: **9 knots**
Machinery: **twin screws, diesel/electric motors; 2900/1800hp**	Armament: **10 550mm (21.7in) TT; one 10mm (3.9in) gun**
Length: **78.25m (256ft 7in)**	Surface range: **4262km (2300nm) at 7.5 knots**
Beam: **6.84m (22ft 6in)**	Crew: **54**
Draught: **5.10m (16ft 9in)**	Launch date: **9 May 1925**

One of the nine Requin- ("Shark"-) class submarines, *Narval* was a large boat that was intended for colonial service, long-range operations against commerce and scouting operations for the fleet. She was on station in the Mediterranean at the outbreak of World War II.

From 10 June 1940, the day Italy entered the war, she made several sorties from Tunisian ports in search of Italian shipping, but failed to make contact. On 1 July, while on war patrol, her captain was ordered by the French Naval Staff to make for the port of Toulon, where French warships were assembling in the newly created Free (Vichy) Zone under the terms of the Franco-German Armistice. He refused, and instead sailed for Malta, where *Narval* was incorporated into the Free French Naval Forces.

On 15 December 1940, *Narval* was sunk by a mine off Tunisia. It is sometimes erroneously recorded that she was sunk off Tobruk by the Italian torpedo boat *Clio* on 7 January 1941.

In January 1944, the name *Narval* was allocated to the former Italian second-class submarine *Bronzo* (shown above), which had been captured by the Royal Navy in July 1943 and later handed over to the Free French. She was used as an asdic training vessel.

ORPHEE

The Diane-class submarine *Orphee* was one of nine in that class, all completed between September 1932 and December 1934. In April 1940, together with other boats of the 10th French Submarine Flotilla and their depot ship *Jules Verne*, *Orphee* deployed to Harwich to reinforce the submarines of the British Home Fleet, beginning operations off the Dutch coast in May of that year.

Early in June 1940, following Italy's entry into the war, *Orphee* deployed to Casablanca, and so managed to escape seizure by the British. During the Allied landings in North Africa in November 1942, when four boats of the Diane class were sunk and *Diane* herself was scuttled, *Orphee* was at sea, and subsequently returned to Casablanca when the fighting was at an end.

Taken over by the Free French Navy, *Orphee* was rearmed and turned over to special duties work, carrying out many clandestine operations, including the landing and extraction of agents in the Mediterranean area. On 7 December 1943 she sank the patrol boat *Faucon* at the entrance to Toulon harbour.

Orphee survived the war and was broken up in 1946. Her two remaining sister vessels, *Antiope* and *Amazone*, were scrapped immediately after the war.

SPECIFICATIONS

ORPHEE

Displacement surfaced: **580tnes (571t)**	Performance surfaced: **13.7 knots**
Displacement submerged: **822tnes (809t)**	Performance submerged: **9.2 knots**
Machinery: **twin screws, diesel/electric motors; 1300/1800hp**	Armament: **six 550mm (21.7in) TT; one 75mm (3in) gun**
Length: **64.4m (211ft 4in)**	Surface range: **7400km (4000nm) at 10 knots**
Beam: **6.2m (20ft 4in)**	Crew: **41**
Draught: **4.3m (14ft 1in)**	Launch date: **10 November 1931**

PONCELET

SPECIFICATIONS

PONCELET

Displacement surfaced: **1595tnes (1570t)**	Performance surfaced: **17–20 knots**
Displacement submerged: **2117tnes (2084t)**	Performance submerged: **10 knots**
Machinery: **twin screws, diesel/electric motors; 2900/1800hp**	Armament: **nine 550mm (21.7in) and two 400mm (15.7in) TT; one 100mm (3.9in) gun**
Length: **92.3m (210ft)**	Surface range: **18,530km (10,000nm) at 10 knots**
Beam: **8.2m (18ft 7in)**	Crew: **61**
Draught: **4.7m (10ft 9in)**	Launch date: **2 February 1935**

At the beginning of World War II, together with the other Redoutable-class submarines *Agosta*, *Ouessant* and *Persee*, *Poncelet* (Cdr de Saussine) was deployed to the Azores for missions against German blockade runners operating in the area.

Poncelet had an early success when, on 28 September 1939, she captured the 5994-tonne (5900-ton) cargo ship *Chemnitz*. In August and September 1940 *Poncelet* acted in support of land operations by the Vichy French government in Libreville, Gabon, where Free French elements were attempting to take over the colonial administration.

The attempted coup failed, but in November Libreville was assaulted by troops of the French Foreign Legion under General Leclerc, supported by Free French and Royal Navy warships. In the course of this action *Poncelet* made a sortie against the Allied ships and was severely damaged by depth-charges from the British sloop HMS *Milford Haven* and, as a result, was forced to surface. Her crew scuttled her and abandoned ship, although Cdr de Saussine chose to remain on board and went down with his submarine.

Poncelet was named after General Jean-Victor Poncelet (1788–1867), the author of many works on applied mechanics.

REQUIN

The Requin ("Shark") class of nine ocean-going boats formed an important element in France's submarine strength at the outbreak of World War II, although the French boats were not all up to 1939 naval warfare standards. *Requin*'s sister submarine *Narval*, for example, reputedly had the noisiest machinery of any boat.

The strength of France's submarine force lay in its sheer size; in September 1939 France had 77 boats in commission, of which 38 were ocean-going, 32 coastal, 6 minelaying and 1 (*Surcouf*) a cruiser. Successive French governments, between the two world wars, regarded submarines as the cheapest way of exercising sea power; the dubious theory was that any nation that had a sufficient number was bound to have a degree of international influence, so planning got off to a rapid start with the Requin class, France's first post-World War I ocean-going submarines.

Requin and most of the others formed part of the Vichy French Navy after the fall of France. On 8 December 1942 she was captured at Bizerta by a small German battle group. Handed over to the Italians and designated *FR113*, she was being converted as a supply submarine when she was again seized by the Germans after Italy's surrender. She was scuttled, then later raised and scrapped.

SPECIFICATIONS

REQUIN

Displacement surfaced: **1168tnes (1150t)**	Performance surfaced: **15 knots**
Displacement submerged: **1464tnes (1441t)**	Performance submerged: **9 knots**
Machinery: **twin screws, diesel/electric motors; 2900/1800hp**	Armament: **10 533mm (21in) TT; one 100mm (3.9in) gun**
Length: **78.2m (56ft 9in)**	Surface range: **10,469km (5650nm) at 10 knots**
Beam: **6.8m (22ft 5in)**	Crew: **54**
Draught: **5m (16ft 9in)**	Launch date: **19 July 1926**

RUBIS

SPECIFICATIONS

RUBIS

Displacement surfaced: 640tnes (630t)	**Performance surfaced:** 13.5 knots
Displacement submerged: 640tnes (630t)	**Performance submerged:** 7.5 knots
Machinery: two screws, diesel/electric motors; 1300/1000hp	**Armament:** 10 533mm (21in) TT; one 100mm (3.9in) gun
Length: 63.4m (208ft 11in)	**Surface range:** 4262km (2300nm) at 7.5 knots
Beam: 5.2m (17ft)	**Crew:** 41
Draught: 3.61m (11ft 9in)	**Launch date:** 23 May 1929

Without doubt the most active and successful minelaying submarine of World War II, *Rubis* (Ruby) was one of six vessels of the Saphir class. Two of the boats were authorized in 1925, and one in each year from 1926 to 1929. They were not outstanding boats, and the key to their success was the safe and effective system of vertical external minelaying tubes, which has been developed by Normand-Fenaux. These were incorporated in the outer ballast tanks and equipped with a direct release mechanism.

In April 1940, following the German invasion of Norway, *Rubis* was one of the French submarine flotilla deployed to Harwich to work alongside Royal Navy boats. *Rubis* joined 11 French submarines of the 10th Flotilla and the 2nd Submarine Division in reinforcing British submarines at Harwich, and she began minelaying operations off Norway on 10 May, operating mainly from the Scottish port of Dundee. In July 1940, after the fall of France, *Rubis*' commanding officer and crew elected to serve with the Free French Naval Forces.

In the course of 22 sorties to Norwegian waters and the Bay of Biscay, *Rubis*' mine barrages sank 14 merchant vessels and eight small warships; she also torpedoed and sank the Finnish merchant ship *Hogland*. She was stricken in 1949.

SURCOUF

An experimental submarine, of a type that was unlikely to be repeated, *Surcouf* was designed for long-range commerce raiding, being described as a "Corsair submarine" by the French Admiralty.

The heaviest submarine in the world at the outbreak of World War II, she carried the largest calibre of guns permitted to be mounted on submarines under the terms of the Washington Treaty; they were identical to those mounted on heavy cruisers, and were mounted in a watertight turret. They had a maximum theoretical range of range of 27,450m (30,000yd) at a 30-degree elevation, although this was reduced to 12,000m (13,000yd) in practice by the limitations of the rangefinder. The guns could be ready to fire two minutes after surfacing.

In July 1940, having sought refuge in Plymouth, *Surcouf* was seized by the British. She later served with the Free French Naval Forces, carrying out patrols in the Atlantic and taking part in the capture of the islands of St Pierre and Miquelon off Newfoundland, which were opposed to General de Gaulle's French government in exile.

Surcouf was lost on 18 February 1942, in an ignominious collision with the US merchant ship *Thomson Lykes* in the Gulf of Mexico.

SPECIFICATIONS

SURCOUF

Displacement surfaced: **3302tnes (3250t)**	Performance surfaced: **18 knots**
Displacement submerged: **4373tnes (4304t)**	Performance submerged: **8.5 knots**
Machinery: **twin screws, diesel/electric motors; 7600/3400hp**	Armament: **eight 551mm (21.7in) and four 400mm (15.75in) TT; two 203mm (8in) guns,**
Length: **110m (360ft 10in)**	Surface range: **18,530km (10,000nm)**
Beam: **9.1m (29ft 9in)**	Crew: **118**
Draught: **9.07m (29ft 9in)**	Launch date: **18 October 1929**

U-30

SPECIFICATIONS

U-30

Displacement surfaced: **640tnes (630t)**	Performance surfaced: **16 knots**
Displacement submerged: **757tnes (745t)**	Performance submerged: **8 knots**
Machinery: **two screws, diesel/electric motors; 2100/750hp**	Armament: **five 533mm (21in) TT; one 88mm (3.5in) gun; one 20mm AA**
Length: **64.5m (211ft 6in)**	Surface range: **6916km (3732nm) at 12 knots**
Beam: **5.8m (19ft 3in)**	Crew: **44**
Draught: **4.4m (14ft 6in)**	Launch date: **1937**

The Type VIIA U-boat *U-30* was among the first wave of German submarines to be deployed to their operational areas in the North Atlantic just prior to the outbreak of World War II. Commanded by Lt Lemp, *U-30* was to become notorious for sinking the passenger liner *Athenia*, which Lemp mistook for an armed merchant cruiser, on 3 September 1939. Lemp sank two more merchant ships on his first war patrol, and on 28 December he torpedoed and damaged the battleship HMS *Barham*.

During the German invasion of Norway in April 1940 the *U-30* supported the German landing at Trondheim, and in July 1940 she became the first German submarine to deploy to the newly captured French base of Lorient.

In the course of several war voyages Lemp destroyed a respectable tonnage of Allied shipping before *U-30* was relegated to training duties. She was scuttled at Flensburg, northern Germany, on 5 May 1945.

After leaving *U-30* Lemp went on to command the *U-110*, losing his life when this submarine was captured by British warships, yielding at the same time a top-secret "Enigma" code machine. These German naval codes, deciphered by Allied specialists, played a major part in defeating the U-boat packs.

U-32

The Type VIIA *U-32* began her war career as part of the U-boats' East Command, operating in the Baltic in support of operations in Poland. Transferred to the North Atlantic theatre towards the end of 1939, and commanded by Lt Jenisch, *U-32* was employed on minelaying duties off the Scottish coast, Portsmouth, Liverpool and Newport. Her mine barrages are known to have claimed at least two merchant ships, and she sank two merchant vessels more in torpedo attacks in March 1940.

Operating from Lorient, *U-32* sank a further five ships on one patrol in July 1940 and six more in August. On 1 September, Jenisch carried out a successful torpedo attack on the cruiser *Fiji* west of the Hebrides, damaging the warship and forcing her to make for port. A further eight merchant ships fell victim to *U-32*'s torpedoes and gunfire in September and October 1940.

On 28 October, *U-32* attacked the passenger ship *Empress of Britain*, which had already been damaged by air attack and under tow, and sank her with two torpedoes north-west of Donegal Bay, Ireland. Two days later, in an attack on a convoy *U-32* was depth-charged and sunk by the British destroyers *Harvester* and *Highlander*.

SPECIFICATIONS

U-32

Displacement surfaced: 636tnes (626t)	**Performance surfaced:** 16 knots
Displacement submerged: 757tnes (745t)	**Performance submerged:** 8 knots
Machinery: two screws, diesel/electric motors; 2100/750hp	**Armament:** five 533mm (21in) TT; one 88mm (3.5in) gun; one 20mm AA
Length: 64.5m (211ft 6in)	**Surface range:** 6916km (3732nm) at 12 knots
Beam: 5.8m (19ft 3in)	**Crew:** 44
Draught: 4.4m (14ft 6in)	**Launch date:** 1937

U-39

SPECIFICATIONS

U-39

Displacement surfaced:
640tnes (630t)

Displacement submerged:
757tnes (745t)

Machinery:
two screws,
diesel/electric motors;
2100/750hp

Length:
64.5m
(211ft 6in)

Beam:
5.8m (19ft 3in)

Draught:
4.4m (14ft 6in)

Performance surfaced:
16 knots

Performance submerged:
8 knots

Armament:
five 533mm (21in) TT;
one 88mm (3.5in) gun;
one 20mm AA

Surface range:
6916km (3732nm)
at 12 knots

Crew:
44

Launch date:
1937

The Type VII U-boat *U-39*, under the command of Lt-Cdr Glattes, came close to achieving a spectacular success in the first month of World War II.

U-boats operating from the north German ports were heavily engaged in minelaying operations during the early weeks of the war. These operations were taking a growing toll of Allied shipping, and to counter them the Royal Navy formed two hunting groups, each comprising an aircraft carrier and four destroyers.

On 14 September 1939, *U-39* sighted the British aircraft carrier *Ark Royal* and her hunting group to the west of the Hebrides and Glattes fired a salvo of three torpedoes at her. Fortunately for the carrier, the torpedoes were of a new type fitted with magnetic pistols. These were faulty and the torpedoes detonated prematurely.

Ark Royal's escorting destroyers, *Faulknor*, *Foxhound* and *Firedrake*, closed in and forced the U-boat to the surface with depth-charges. Her crew escaped just before she sank and were taken prisoner.

Just three days later, *U-39's* sister boat, *U-29*, sank the aircraft carrier *Courageous*, with the loss of 514 lives. After that, the Royal Navy withdrew carriers from its anti-U-boat operations.

U-47

The *U-47* was one of 24 Type VIIB U-boats, the Type VIIB being a slightly larger version of the Type VIIA, with a greater range and slightly higher surface speed.

Commanded by Lt-Cdr Gunther Prien, the *U-47* achieved early fame in World War II when, on the night of 13/14 October 1939, having already sunk three British merchant ships, she penetrated the defences of Scapa Flow and made a daring attack on the 29,616-tonne (29,150-ton) Royal Sovereign-class battleship *Royal Oak*, a veteran of World War I, and sank her with three torpedo hits.

The attack cost the lives of more than 800 British seamen and came as a considerable blow to British morale. Prien and his crew, understandably feted as heroes by the German people, operated in support of the German invasion of Norway in April 1940 and subsequently deployed to the French Atlantic ports, where they continued to operate against British Atlantic convoys.

This excellent U-boat commander and his highly trained crew sank a further 27 ships before being lost when *U-47* was surprised in a heavy squall and depth-charged by the Royal Navy corvettes *Arbutus* and *Camellia* on the night of 7/8 March 1941.

SPECIFICATIONS

U-47

Displacement surfaced: **765tnes (753t)**	*Performance surfaced:* **17.25 knots**
Displacement submerged: **871tnes (857t)**	*Performance submerged:* **8 knots**
Machinery: **two shafts, diesel/electric motors; 2800/750hp**	*Armament:* **10 533mm (21in) TT; one 100mm (3.9in) gun**
Length: **66.5m (218ft)**	*Surface range:* **4262km (2300nm) at 7.5 knots**
Beam: **6.2m (20ft 3in)**	*Crew:* **44**
Draught: **4.7m (15ft 6in)**	*Launch date:* **1938**

U-81

SPECIFICATIONS

U-81

Displacement surfaced: **793tnes (781t)**	Performance surfaced: **17 knots**
Displacement submerged: **879tnes (871t)**	Performance submerged: **7.5 knots**
Machinery: **two shafts, diesel/electric motors; 2800/750hp**	Armament: **five 533mm (21in) TT; one 37mm (3.5in) gun; one 20mm AA**
Length: **66.5m (218ft)**	Surface range: **10,454km (5642nm) at 12 knots**
Beam: **6.2m (20ft 3in)**	Crew: **44**
Draught: **4.7m (15ft 6in)**	Launch date: **1939**

The British aircraft carrier *Ark Royal* eventually succumbed to German torpedoes, but not until November 1941, and the submarine that launched them was the *U-81*.

Under the command of Lt-Cdr Guggenberger, this Type VIIC boat began operations in the Arctic in July 1941 and narrowly escaped being sunk by a Soviet patrol vessel on her first sortie. She continued to operate in the Arctic as part of the 'Markgraf' U-boat group before deploying to the Mediterranean in October of that year.

On 13 November 1941, *Ark Royal* was returning to Gibraltar after flying off reinforcement fighters for Malta when she was attacked by *U-81*, being hit by one torpedo from a salvo of four. Despite desperate attempts to tow her to safety, she sank the following day, fortunately with the loss of only one life.

U-81 continued to operate in the Mediterranean, but did not enjoy any further success until November 1942, when she sank a transport vessel during the Allied landings in North Africa. The boat now had a new commander, Lt Krieg, but failed to achieve any major successes, her principal victims being sailing vessels, which were sunk by gunfire.

On 9 January 1944, *U-81* was destroyed in an air attack on Pola, her main operating base.

U-106

Designed for long-range operations in distant waters, the Type IXB U-boats, of which *U-106* was one, were a development of the Type IXAs but with an increased radius. Some Type IXBs were provided with extra fuel tankage, giving them enough range (16,100km [8700nm] at 12 knots) to deploy as far as Japan (presumably to attack British vessels).

Operating from bases such as Penang and Singapore, these Type IXB boats were a constant threat to Allied convoys in the Indian Ocean. The *U-106*, however, spent her entire war in the Atlantic, beginning operations early in 1941. From time to time she acted as a weather boat, her range enabling her to operate far out in the ocean.

During this period (February to April 1941) the *U-106* enjoyed considerable success under her able captain, Lt-Cdr Oesten; on the night of 19/20 March she torpedoed the battleship *Malaya*, which was escorting a convoy in the central Atlantic, causing sufficient damage to remove her from first-line service for the rest of the war.

The *U-106* continued on operations under a new captain, Lt-Cdr Rasch, and achieved further sinkings before she herself was sunk by air attack off Cape Ortegal, Biscay, on 2 August 1943.

SPECIFICATIONS

U-106

Displacement surfaced: **1068tnes (1051t)**	Performance surfaced: **18.25 knots**
Displacement submerged: **2183tnes (1178t)**	Performance submerged: **7.25 knots**
Machinery: **two shafts, diesel/electric motors; 4400/1000hp**	Armament: **six 533mm (21in) TT; one 102mm (4.1in)**
Length: **76.5m (251ft)**	Surface range: **13,993km (7552nm)**
Beam: **6.8m (22ft 3in)**	Crew: **48**
Draught: **4.6m (15ft)**	Launch date: **1939**

U-110

SPECIFICATIONS

U-110

Displacement surfaced: **1068tnes (1051t)**	Performance surfaced: **18.25 knots**
Displacement submerged: **2183tnes (1178t)**	Performance submerged: **7.25 knots**
Machinery: **two shafts, diesel/electric motors; 4400/1000hp**	Armament: **six 533mm (21in) TT; one 102mm (4.1in) gun; one 20mm AA**
Length: **76.5m (251ft)**	Surface range: **13,993km (7552nm)**
Beam: **6.8m (22ft 3in)**	Crew: **48**
Draught: **4.6m (15ft)**	Launch date: **1939**

On the evening of 15 March 1941, the Type IXB submarine *U-110* under the command of Lt-Cdr Julius Lemp (formerly of the *U-30*) closed in to attack a British convoy in the North Atlantic, together with several other U-boats. These included two commanded by German U-boat "aces": the *U-99* (Lt-Cdr Kretschmer) and the *U-100* (Lt-Cdr Schepke). In what turned out to be a particularly disastrous encounter with Royal Navy escort forces, *U-99* and *U-100* were both sunk, while *U-110* and the others were beaten off.

For the German submariners, it was a taste of things to come, and an indication of what a properly organized escort group could achieve.

Lemp and his crew finally met their fate on 9 May of that year, when the *U-110* closed in to make an attack on convoy HX123, south of Iceland. Lemp succeeded in sinking two ships, but depth-charges from the corvette *Aubretia* blew the *U-110* to the surface and she was abandoned by her crew, being captured intact by a boarding party from the destroyer *Bulldog*.

The British sailors seized an "Enigma" code machine and other material that was to prove priceless to British intelligence, shortly before the *U-110* sank under tow. Lt-Cdr Lemp lost his life in this incident.

U-112

The design of the Type XI U-boat *U-112* had its origins in World War I, when the German Navy enjoyed considerable success with its so-called "submarine cruisers". These were large, heavily armed boats whose tactics were to surface and sink merchant vessels with gunfire (as shown above), reserving their torpedoes for armoured warships that were able to defend themselves.

The result was that German submarines carried progressively heavier armament as their design evolved during the war years, until eventually, boats of new construction carried two 150mm (5.9in) guns and older boats were modified to bring them up to a similar standard. Guns of this calibre had a greater range than any that were mounted in merchant vessels, so the U-boat commander could stand off and sink his victim at leisure.

The concept of the submarine cruiser, which was intended for surface attacks against merchant shipping, was resurrected in World War II with the design of the German Type XI. As with the French *Surcouf*, of similar concept, provision was made for a spotter aircraft. Three boats were planned, beginning with *U-112*, but they never progressed beyond the project stage, and it was left to the Japanese to develop comparable vessels.

SPECIFICATIONS

U-112

Displacement surfaced: **3190tnes (3140t)**	*Performance surfaced:* **23 knots**
Displacement submerged: **3688tnes (3630t)**	*Performance submerged:* **7 knots**
Machinery: **two shafts, diesel/electric motors**	*Armament:* **eight 533mm (21in) TT; four 127mm (5in) guns; two 30mm and two 20mm AA**
Length: **115m (377ft)**	*Surface range:* **25,266km (13,635nm) at 12 knots**
Beam: **9.5m (31ft)**	*Crew:* **110**
Draught: **6m (20ft)**	*Launch date:* **Projected only**

U-570

SPECIFICATIONS

U-570

Displacement surfaced: **793tnes (781t)**	Performance surfaced: **17 knots**
Displacement submerged: **879tnes (871t)**	Performance submerged: **7.5 knots**
Machinery: **two shafts, diesel/electric motors; 2800/750hp**	Armament: **five 533mm (21in) TT; one 37mm (3.5in) gun; one 20mm AA**
Length: **66.5m (218ft)**	Surface range: **10,454km (5642nm) at 12 knots**
Beam: **6.2m (20ft 3in)**	Crew: **44**
Draught: **4.7m (15ft 6in)**	Launch date: **1939**

On 27 August 1941 the Type VIIC submarine *U-570*, commanded by Lt Hans Rahmlow, was one of a group of U-boats operating southwest of Iceland against convoy HX145, which had been located by the German Signals Intelligence Service.

The submarine was attacked in bad weather by a Lockheed Hudson of No 269 Squadron RAF, flown by Sqn Ldr J.H. Thompson, and damaged; Rahmlow, unable to submerge, raised the flag of surrender and continued to circle the boat until relieved by a Catalina of No 209 Squadron. The armed trawler *Northern Chief* reached the scene that evening, followed by three more trawlers and the destroyers *Burwell* and *Niagara* the following day.

The submarine's crew was taken off and the *U-570* was towed to Iceland, where she was beached. Although her crew had destroyed most of the secret material on board, the capture of an intact U-boat was an important achievement.

Commissioned into the Royal Navy as HMS *Graph*, she was used for depth-charge trials, yielding information on the effects of explosions on her pressure hull. She was wrecked while on passage from Chatham to the Clyde in March 1944 and was scrapped in 1947.

U-791

In the early 1930s, the German engineer Helmuth Walter began work on a circuit motor that would function independently of oxygen derived from the atmosphere. The turbine he developed used concentrated hydrogen peroxide, which was heated via a catalyst to produce the required oxygen and high-pressure steam.

The first experimental submarine fitted with this revolutionary system, V80, was launched in January 1940 and reached the then incredible submerged speed of 28 knots.

Other experimental boats followed, culminating in the Type V300 experimental submarine *U-791*, built in 1943. However, work proceeded very slowly, not least because of problems in handling the highly unstable hydrogen peroxide and in designing an effective streamlined hull in order to achieve the desired underwater speeds. As a consequence the entire project was given low priority.

By 1943, when conventional U-boats were being defeated by Allied countermeasures in the Atlantic and Mediterranean, work was at last accelerated, but by then it was too late; it was calculated that the development of an operational long-range Walter-propelled submarine would have taken at least two years.

SPECIFICATIONS

U-791

Displacement surfaced: **609tnes (600t)**	*Performance surfaced:* **9.3 knots**
Displacement submerged: **655tnes (645t)**	*Performance submerged:* **19 knots**
Machinery: **single screw, two diesels and two Walter turbines and two electric motors; 150/2180/75hp**	*Armament:* **two 533mm (21in) TT**
Length: **52.10m (170ft 11in)**	*Surface range:* **not known**
Beam: **4.00m (13ft 1in)**	*Crew:* **25**
Draught: **5.50m (70ft)**	*Launch date:* **1943**

U-1405

SPECIFICATIONS

U-1405

Displacement surfaced:
319tnes (314t)

Displacement submerged:
363tnes (357t)

Machinery:
single screw, two diesels and two Walter turbines and two electric motors; 150/2180/75hp

Length:
39.5m (129ft 7in)

Beam:
3.4m (11ft 2in)

Draught:
4.7m (15ft 5in)

Performance surfaced:
8.5 knots (estimated)

Performance submerged:
23 knots

Armament:
Two 533mm (21in) TT

Surface range:
4825km (2604nm) (estimated)

Crew:
19

Launch date:
Project cancelled

The first operational Walter-powered boats were designated Type XVIIB. Five units were launched between 1944 and 1945 but only three, *U-1405*, *U-1406* and *U-1407*, were completed. All three were scuttled in May 1945; one of them, the *U-1407*, was salved, repaired and allocated to the Royal Navy under the name *Meteorite*. She was used to make exhaustive tests of the Walter propulsion system and was scrapped in 1950, by which time nuclear reactors were under investigation as submarine propulsion systems.

The Type XVIIBs were to have been followed by 10 Type XVIIGs, led by *U-1081*. Although the Walter turbine was their primary propulsion system, they retained diesel and electric motors to extend their overall combat radius.

The Type XVIIG class were generally similar to the Type XVIIB, although very slightly smaller. A further class of experimental boats, the Type XVIIK, was planned for the purpose of testing the closed-cycle diesel engine as an alternative to the Walter turbine, but like the XVIIG it never advanced beyond project stage.

There is little doubt that the Walter boats, had they been available two or three years earlier, would have made an enormous difference to the outcome of the Battle of the Atlantic.

U-2321

The *U-2321* was the first of the small Type XXIII electric-powered coastal submarines, which were the subject of a top-priority construction programme that took place in bomb-proof bunkers in the latter months of World War II.

Fitted with electric "creeping" motors, these Type XXIII boats were very quiet and hard to detect. Construction of this class was originally intended to go ahead at various locations, notably Hamburg, Kiel, Toulon, Genoa, Monfalcone and Nikolayev, but because of the rapid contraction of the German fronts in 1944 as the Wehrmacht suffered a series of defeats, building took place only at the German ports.

In total, 63 units were commissioned, of which 51 were either at sea or in various stages of construction when the war came to an end. The Type XXIII building programme was also seriously disrupted and delayed by Allied bombing.

The *U-2321*, commanded by Lt Barschkies, deployed to Kristiansand, Norway, and made her first war patrol off the Scottish coast in March 1945, sinking one small freighter. Together with other Type XXIIIs, she was surrendered in May 1945.

Many other Type XXIIIs, in defiance of the terms of surrender, were scuttled by their crews instead.

SPECIFICATIONS

U-2321

Displacement surfaced: **236tnes (232t)**	*Performance surfaced:* **9.75 knots**
Displacement submerged: **260tnes (256t)**	*Performance submerged:* **12.5 knots**
Powerplant: **single-shaft diesel/electric motors plus silent creeping electric motor; 580/580/35hp**	*Armament:* **two 533mm (21in) TT**
Length: **34m (112ft)**	*Surface range:* **2171km (1172nm)**
Beam: **2.9m (9ft 9in)**	*Crew:* **14**
Draught: **3.7m (12ft 3in)**	*Launch date:* **Not known**

U-2501

SPECIFICATIONS

U-2501

Displacement surfaced: 1647tnes (1621t)	**Performance surfaced:** 15.5 knots
Displacement submerged: 2100tnes (2067t)	**Performance submerged:** 16 knots
Powerplant: twin screws, diesel/electric motors, silent creeping motors; 4000/5000/226hp at 15/15/5 knots	**Armament:** six 533mm (21in) TT; four 30mm AA guns
Length: 77m (251ft 8in)	**Surface range:** 17934km (9678nm)
Beam: 8m (26ft 3in)	**Crew:** 57
Draught: 6.2m (20ft 4in)	**Launch date:** 1944

In 1943, with U-boats beginning to suffer serious losses, and with no prospect of the new Walter boats making an early operational debut, the German Admiralty decided on an expedient by marrying conventional submarine machinery to the new streamlined hull design.

The result was the Type XXI "electro-boat", which had a redesigned internal hull in order to provide room for more batteries, raising the underwater speed to 15 knots. The boats were fitted with "creeper" engines, for silent underwater escape at five knots.

Other innovations included a fast mechanical reloading system for the six bow torpedo tubes, a retractable Schnorchel fitted with radar warning receivers and other countermeasures devices, an electronic command centre for accurate plotting and tracking of targets, and two remotely controlled 30mm antiaircraft mountings.

The boats were ordered into mass production, with 20 units per month envisaged and an in-service target date of November 1944, but this proved totally unrealistic. In fact, the project was far too late to make a difference to the war. The *U-2501* was the first of the Type XXIs, but she never became operational, being scuttled at Hamburg on 2 May 1945.

U-2511

One of the reasons for the delay in the Type XXI becoming operational was that the boat was so radically different, and more highly capable, than anything that had preceded, and so new handling and attack techniques had to be evaluated. The other main reason was Allied bombing of Germany, which seriously disrupted the building programme.

Of the completed boats, 24 were lost through enemy action or accident. One hundred and twenty-one units were actually commissioned and 55 were deployed to Norway in March 1945 for last-ditch operations against Allied shipping in the North Sea area. Had all of the Type XXIs been used, they might have inflicted massive casualties on the Allies; as it was, their commander never received operational orders for them and an expected last stand of German forces in Norway never took place.

In fact, only two boats, *U-2511* and *U-3008*, made an operational sortie, and this was interrupted by the ending of the war. At that moment the *U-2511*'s captain had actually sighted a British cruiser, but having been advised that a German surrender was imminent, he elected to make only a dummy attack on it. *U-2511* later surrendered at Bergen and was subsequently scrapped.

SPECIFICATIONS

U-2511

Displacement surfaced:
1647tnes (1621t)

Displacement submerged:
2100tnes (2067t)

Machinery:
**twin screws,
diesel/electric motors,
silent creeping motors;
4000/5000/226hp at
15/15/5 knots**

Length:
77m (251ft 8in)

Beam:
8m (26ft 3in)

Draught:
6.2m (20ft 4in)

Performance surfaced:
15.5 knots

Performance submerged:
16 knots

Armament:
**six 533mm (21in) TT;
four 30mm AA guns**

Surface range:
17,934km (9678nm)

Crew:
57

Launch date:
1944

CLYDE

SPECIFICATIONS

CLYDE

Displacement surfaced: **1834tnes (1805t)**	Performance surfaced: **21.75 knots**
Displacement submerged: **2680tnes (2723t)**	Performance submerged: **10 knots**
Machinery: **two screws, diesel/electric motors; 10,000/2500hp**	Armament: **eight 533mm (21in) TT; one 100mm (4in) gun**
Length: **99.1m (325ft)**	Surface range: **9265km (5000nm) at 10 knots**
Beam: **8.5m (28ft)**	Crew: **61**
Draught: **4.1m (13ft 6in)**	Launch date: **26 January 1932**

HMS *Clyde* was one of three Thames class combined fleet and patrol type submarines laid down between 1932 and 1933 and completed between 1932 and 1935. There were originally to have been 20 boats in this class, but the order was drastically reduced following a policy change. The boats featured a double hull with welded external fuel tanks, eliminating the leakage problems that had plagued earlier classes. *Clyde*, *Thames* and the third boat, *Severn*, were assigned to the 2nd Submarine Flotilla on the outbreak of World War II, beginning operations against enemy shipping in the North Sea and off the coast of Norway.

On 20 June 1940 *Clyde*, under Lt-Cdr Ingram, obtained a torpedo hit on the bow of the German battlecruiser *Gneisenau*, which had left Trondheim to make a sortie into the Iceland-Faeroes passage. The warship limped back to Trondheim and, following temporary repairs, sailed for Kiel where she remained until early 1941. This was a major success, as the German vessel was a fast and powerfully armed ship. *Clyde*'s sister boat *Thames* fell victim to a mine off Norway on 23 July 1940. After many successful forays against enemy shipping in northern waters, both boats deployed to the Eastern Fleet via the Mediterranean in 1944 and were scrapped in India in 1946.

OBERON

Laid down in 1924 at Chatham Dockyard, HM submarine *Oberon* was in many respects an experimental craft. Based on the L class, which made its appearance in the final year of World War I, she was originally designated *O1* and had a number of advanced design features, including welded fuel tanks that replaced the earlier riveted ones during the course of a refit.

Oberon had a design depth limit of 150m (500ft), but her design performances were never attained. However, she had a good radius of action, which would have made her ideal for service in Far Eastern waters, as was originally intended.

Oberon was followed into service by two more boats, *Otway* and *Oxley*, which were built by Vickers and were similar to *Oberon* except for some improvements in hull form, which were designed to give a higher speed. Both boats were laid down for the Royal Australian Navy, being returned to Britain in 1931. *Oxley* was accidentally torpedoed by HM submarine *Triton* on 10 September 1939, just 10 days after the start of World War II. *Oberon* saw war service in home waters and *Otway* in the Mediterranean. Both were broken up in 1945. The Odin class, six of which were completed in 1928, contained further improvements on the *Oberon* design.

SPECIFICATIONS

OBERON

Displacement surfaced: **1513tnes (1490t)**	*Performance surfaced:* **15.5 knots**
Displacement submerged: **1922tnes (1892t)**	*Performance submerged:* **9 knots**
Machinery: **twin screws, diesel/electric motors; 3000/1350hp**	*Armament:* **eight 533mm (21in) TT; one 100mm (4in) gun**
Length: **83.4m (273ft 8in)**	*Surface range:* **9500km (5633nm)**
Beam: **8.3m (27ft 3in)**	*Crew:* **54**
Draught: **4.6m (15ft)**	*Launch date:* **24 September 1926**

ORPHEUS

SPECIFICATIONS

ORPHEUS

Displacement surfaced: 1513tnes (1490t)	**Performance surfaced:** 15.5 knots
Displacement submerged: 1922tnes (1892t)	**Performance submerged:** 9 knots
Machinery: twin screws, diesel/electric motors; 4400/1320hp	**Armament:** eight 533mm (21in) TT; one 100mm (4in) gun
Length: 83.4m (273ft 8in)	**Surface range:** 9500km (5633nm)
Beam: 8.3m (27ft 3in)	**Crew:** 54
Draught: 4.6m (15ft)	**Launch date:** 26 February 1929

Orpheus was the last in the batch of six Odin-class submarines completed for the Royal Navy between 1929 and 1930. As with *Oberon*, the design depth limit was 150m (500ft), although operationally the boats were capable of diving to 109m (360ft). Diving trials showed that some stiffening of the hull was necessary.

Together with the class leaders, *Odin*, *Olympus* and *Otus*, *Orpheus* saw service on the East India station before being transferred to the Mediterranean Fleet in 1940, at the time of Italy's entry into World War II. Bad luck seemed to follow this class of submarine.

Odin was the first of the Odin-class boats to become a victim of enemy action. On 14 June 1940, while operating out of Malta, she was sunk in the Gulf of Taranto by the Italian destroyer *Strale*. Two more losses came in swift succession: *Orpheus* was sunk off Tobruk by the destroyer *Turbine* on 16 June 1940, while *Oswald* was sunk by the destroyer *Vivaldi* south of Calabria on 1 August 1940. A fourth boat, *Olympus*, was lost when she ran into a mine barrage during a sortie from Malta on 8 May 1942.

The two other Odin-class boats, *Osiris* and *Otus*, were both fitted with a 20mm Oerlikon gun. They survived the war and were scrapped at Durban in September 1946.

PROTEUS

The six vessels of the Parthian class, of which HM submarine *Proteus* was the sole survivor at the end of World War II, were similar to those of the Odin class, but featured an altered bow shape. All six boats in the class were laid down in 1928 and completed between 1930 and 1931. Each was fitted with Vulcan clutches and high-capacity batteries, although output was later reduced.

These Parthian-class boats were the first submarines to carry the more potent Mk VIII torpedo, which became standard armament on all subsequent British submarines of that period.

One of the boats, *Poseidon*, was lost in a collision in June 1931. At the outbreak of World War II the remaining five were on the China station, but were deployed to the Mediterranean in 1940 to help counter the threat posed by the powerful Italian fleet.

Phoenix was sunk by the Italian torpedo-boat *Albatros* off Sicily on 16 July 1940; *Perseus* was torpedoed by the Italian submarine *Enrico Toti* off Zante on 6 December 1941; *Pandora* was bombed by Italian aircraft at Malta on 1 April 1942; and *Parthian* failed to return from a sortie to the Adriatic on 11 August 1943, the probable victim of an Italian mine.

Proteus was later relegated to a training role and was broken up in 1964.

SPECIFICATIONS

PROTEUS

Displacement surfaced: **1788tnes (1760t)**	*Performance surfaced:* **17.5 knots**
Displacement submerged: **2072tnes (2040t)**	*Performance submerged:* **8.6 knots**
Machinery: **two screws, diesel/electric motors; 4640/1635hp**	*Armament:* **10 533mm (21in) TT; one 100mm (3.9in) gun**
Length: **88.14m (289ft 2in)**	*Surface range:* **4262km (2300nm) at 7.5 knots**
Beam: **9.12m (29ft 11in)**	*Crew:* **53**
Draught: **4.85m (15ft 11in)**	*Launch date:* **23 July 1929**

SEAL

SPECIFICATIONS

SEAL

Displacement surfaced: **1524tnes (1500t)**	Performance surfaced: **15 knots**
Displacement submerged: **2086tnes (2053t)**	Performance submerged: **8.75 knots**
Machinery: **twin screws, diesel/electric motors; 3300/1630hp**	Armament: **six 533mm (21in) TT; one 100mm (4in) gun**
Length: **81.5m (267ft)**	Surface range: **10,191km (5500nm) at 10 knots**
Beam: **9m (29ft 9in)**	Crew: **61**
Draught: **13.75m (13ft 9in)**	Launch date: **7 September 1938**

In May 1940, HM submarine *Seal* achieved notoriety by becoming the first and only British submarine to be captured by the Germans.

One of six Porpoise-class boats, *Seal* had just laid a mine barrage in the southern exit of the Kattegat on 5 May 1940 when she was damaged by a mine detonation. Unable to submerge or to scuttle herself, she was forced to surrender to a German Arado 196 floatplane which appeared at first light. She was in the process of deploying to the China Station at the outbreak of war, but was ordered to return to home waters. She never reached them.

After her capture, *Seal* was designated UB in German service, and was later scuttled at Kiel on 3 May 1945.

Of the other boats in the Porpoise class, *Grampus* was sunk by the Italian torpedo-boats *Cl10* and *Circe* off Augusta on 24 June 1940; *Narwhal* failed to return from a sortie into Norwegian waters off Norway in July 1940, possibly having been sunk by a German maritime aircraft; *Cachalot* was rammed by the Italian torpedo-boat *Papa* off Cyrenaica on 4 August 1941; and *Porpoise* was sunk by Japanese air attack in the Malacca Strait on 19 January 1945. *Rorqual* survived the war, and was broken up in 1946.

SERAPH

One of 33 S-class submarines laid down under a war emergency programme initiated in 1941, *Seraph* and her sisters were improved and enlarged developments of the Shark class of the late 1930s. Though they were rushed into service, the class served the Royal Navy well during World War II.

The S class submarines, originally intended for service in the North Sea area, were offensively employed in all three main theatres of war, and proved a most successful design.

Seraph's area of operations was the Mediterranean, where, in addition to normal war patrols, she carried out many special missions, such as inserting agents along enemy coastlines – dangerous but necessary work.

During the Allied invasion of Sicily, in July 1943, *Seraph* acted as beacon submarine for Task Force 85. In July/September 1944 she was converted at Devonport to the high-speed target role, with a streamlined hull and casing, higher-capacity batteries, uprated motors and new propellers. This revised configuration increased her speed at periscope depth by some three knots.

Nine of the S class submarines were lost during World War II and two more boats, *Safari* and *Sportsman*, were lost in post-war accidents – an average loss rate compared to other classes. *Seraph* was broken up in 1965.

SPECIFICATIONS

SERAPH

Displacement surfaced: **886tnes (872t)**	Performance surfaced: **14.75 knots**
Displacement submerged: **1005tnes (990t)**	Performance submerged: **9 knots**
Machinery: **twin screws, diesel/electric motors; 1900/1300hp**	Armament: **six 533mm (21in) TT; one 76mm (3in) gun**
Length: **66.1m (216ft 10in)**	Surface range: **11,400km (6144nm)**
Beam: **7.2m (23ft 8in)**	Crew: **44**
Draught: **3.4m (11ft 2in)**	Launch date: **25 October 1941**

SPLENDID

SPECIFICATIONS

SPLENDID

Displacement surfaced: **886tnes (872t)**	Performance surfaced: **14.75 knots**
Displacement submerged: **1005tnes (990t)**	Performance submerged: **9 knots**
Machinery: **twin screws, diesel/electric motors; 1900/1300hp**	Armament: **six 533mm (21in) TT; one 76mm (3in) gun**
Length: **66.1m (216ft 10in)**	Surface range: **11,400km (6144nm)**
Beam: **7.2m (23ft 8in)**	Crew: **48**
Draught: **3.4m (11ft 2in)**	Launch date: **19 January 1942**

One of the second group of S-class submarines, *Splendid* was originally designated *P.228*. She deployed to the Mediterranean theatre, where she enjoyed some success: in November 1942, commanded by Lt-Cdr McGeogh, she torpedoed the Italian destroyer *Velite* in the Bay of Naples. In the following month she sank another Italian destroyer, the *Aviere*, as well as a 5129-tonne (5048-ton) freighter.

These successes were followed, in January 1943, by the sinking of four merchant vessels totalling 10,225 tonnes (10,064 tons), one of which was the 8058-tonne (7931-ton) *Emma*, in the Tyrrhenian Sea.

These operations by *Splendid* and other British submarines on the main convoy route between Sicily and North Africa severely disrupted Axis attempts to resupply their forces in Tunisia, which were under strong pressure from the British and American armies.

Splendid enjoyed more good fortune against enemy convoys in March 1943, when she sank four more freighters, totalling over 14,224 tonnes (14,000 tons) in the same operational area. The Germans and the Italians heavily reinforced their convoy escorts, and on 21 April 1943 *Splendid* was sunk by the German destroyer *Hermes* (the former Greek *Vasileus Georgios*) off the island of Capri.

SWORDFISH

HM submarine *Swordfish* was the second of four boats in the first group of S-class submarines. There were two groups, totalling 12 boats, and only four were to survive World War II.

Two of the boats that did not survive, *Seahorse* and *Starfish*, were lost within 48 hours of one another on 7 and 9 January 1940, the victims of German minesweepers in the Heligoland Bight.

Of the rest, *Sterlet* was sunk by German trawlers in the Skagerrak on 18 April 1940; *Shark* was also sunk by German minesweepers during a patrol off the Norwegian coast on 6 July 1940; *Salmon* was lost when she struck a mine in the same area two days later; *Spearfish* was torpedoed by *U-34* off Norway on 2 August 1940; *Swordfish* failed to return from a patrol off Ushant on 16 November 1940, possibly sunk by a mine; *Snapper* failed to return from the Bay of Biscay on 12 February 1941, the presumed victim of a mine barrage; and *Sunfish* was bombed in error by British aircraft while on passage to North Russia, having been transferred to the Soviet Navy.

Sturgeon was luckier than the others in her class: she served in home waters until 1943, when she was transferred to the Royal Netherlands Navy as the *Zeehond* (*Seadog*). She was scrapped in 1947.

SPECIFICATIONS

SWORDFISH

Displacement surfaced: 650tnes (640t)	**Performance surfaced:** 15 knots
Displacement submerged: 942tnes (927t)	**Performance submerged:** 10 knots
Machinery: twin shafts, diesel/electric motors; 1550/1440hp	**Armament:** six 533mm (21in) TT; one 76mm (3in) gun
Length: 58.8m (193ft)	**Surface range:** 7412km (4000nm)
Beam: 7.3m (24ft)	**Crew:** 38
Draught: 3.2m (10ft 6in)	**Launch date:** 8 January 1932

THUNDERBOLT

SPECIFICATIONS

THUNDERBOLT

Displacement surfaced: 1107tnes (1090t)	**Performance surfaced:** 15.25 knots
Displacement submerged: 1600tnes (1575t)	**Performance submerged:** 9 knots
Machinery: twin screws, diesel/electric motors; 2500/1450hp	**Armament:** 10 533mm (21in) TT; one 100mm (4in) gun
Length: 80.8m (265ft)	**Surface range:** 7041km (3800nm) at 10 knots
Beam: 8m (26ft 6in)	**Crew:** 59
Draught: 4.5m (14ft 9in)	**Launch date:** 29 June 1938

One of the first group of 15 T-class submarines, *Thunderbolt* had the dubious distinction of being lost twice during her career.

On 1 June 1939, then named HMS *Thetis*, she sank during trials with the loss of all 99 people on board. Salved and refitted, she was renamed *Thunderbolt*. On 15 December 1940, she attacked the Italian submarine *Tarantini*, which subsequently sank, in the Bay of Biscay.

Deployed to the Mediterranean, *Thunderbolt* enjoyed considerable success against Italian shipping, much of her operational time being spent in the Aegean. She also undertook some special missions, most notably on 3 January 1943, when she and another T-class boat, *Trooper*, launched Chariots (human torpedoes) in an attack on Palermo. The Chariot crews laid charges that severely damaged the Italian cruiser *Ulpio Traiano* and a large transport.

Early in 1943 *Thunderbolt* was operating in the Adriatic, where she sank several sailing vessels by gunfire. Returning to convoy attacks on the Sicily-Tunisia route, she was eventually sunk by the Italian corvette *Cicogna* on 24 March 1943.

Of the first 15 T-class submarines, a total of nine were lost in World War II.

UNBROKEN

HM submarine *Unbroken* (*P.42*) was one of the second group of U-class boats built by Vickers-Armstrong, the total output being 51 units. Four of the class were transferred on loan to the Royal Canadian Navy for training purposes and four were sent to the Far East, the remainder operating either in home waters or the Mediterranean.

On 14 August 1942, commanded by Lt Mars, *Unbroken* torpedoed the Italian cruisers *Attendolo* and *Bolzano* off the Aeolian Islands in support of Operation Pedestal, a major effort to resupply the island of Malta. From then on *Unbroken* enjoyed a very successful war career in the Mediterranean under Lt Mars and his successor, Lt Andrew.

On 26 July 1944, together with three other British submarines, *Unbroken* was handed over to the Soviet Navy and renamed as the *V-2*. The submarine remained in Soviet hands until 1949, operating from Murmansk, before returning to Britain to be scrapped in 1950.

The U-class submarines, being smaller than average in size, were able to operate very effectively in shallow coastal waters, and on the approach to harbours.

Seventeen U-class boats were lost on operations during World War II.

SPECIFICATIONS

UNBROKEN

Displacement surfaced: **554tnes (545t)**	Performance surfaced: **11.25 knots**
Displacement submerged: **752tnes (740t)**	Performance submerged: **9 knots**
Machinery: **twin screws, diesel/electric motors; 825/615hp**	Armament: **four 533mm (21in) TT; one 76mm (3in) gun**
Length: **54.9m (180ft)**	Surface range: **7041km (3800nm)**
Beam: **4.8m (16ft)**	Crew: **31**
Draught: **3.8m (12ft 9in)**	Launch date: **4 November 1941**

UPHOLDER

SPECIFICATIONS

UPHOLDER

Displacement surfaced: **554tnes (545t)**	Performance surfaced: **11.25 knots**
Displacement submerged: **752tnes (740t)**	Performance submerged: **9 knots**
Machinery: **two screws, diesel/electric motors; 825/615hp**	Armament: **four 533mm (21in) TT; one 76mm (3in) gun**
Length: **54.9m (180ft)**	Surface range: **7041km (3800nm)**
Beam: **4.8m (16ft)**	Crew: **31**
Draught: **3.8m (12ft 9in)**	Launch date: **8 July 1940**

Another famous U-class submarine, but one that unfortunately did not survive the war, was HMS *Upholder*. Commanded by Lt-Cdr M.D. Wanklyn, she served with the Malta-based 10th Submarine Flotilla, whose boats sank 49 troops transports and supply ships totalling 152,400 tonnes (150,000 tons) from the start of June to the end of September 1941.

In May, Wanklyn was awarded the VC for sinking the Italian liner *Conte Rosso* in a particularly daring attack, and in another successful sortie on 18 September, *Upholder* sank the Italian troop-carrying liners *Neptunia* and *Oceania*, both 19,304 tonnes (19,000 tons).

On 9 November 1941 she torpedoed the Italian destroyer *Libeccio*, which sank under tow the next day, and in January 1942 she sank the Italian submarine *St Bon*, which was being used as a petrol transport.

Other successful operations against enemy convoys followed, and in March she sank the Italian submarine *Tricheco* in the central Mediterranean. Two more Italian submarines, *Guglielmotti* and *Millo*, were sunk in the same action by U-class boats *Ultimatum* and *Unbeaten*.

Upholder's phenomenal run of luck finally ran out on 14 April 1942, when she was sunk by the Italian torpedo boat *Pegaso* on her 24th war mission. She was the Royal Navy's most successful submarine.

UTMOST

Another U-class boat that started its operational career early in 1941 with the 10th Submarine Flotilla was *Utmost*, commanded by Lt-Cdr R.D. Cayley, who opened his score by sinking a freighter north of Triploi on 12 February. He sank another 5550-tonne (5463-ton) vessel on 11 February, and one of similar tonnage on 9 March.

His score continued to mount in the summer of 1941, and a close rivalry developed between the crews of *Utmost* and *Upholder*. On 28 July, *Utmost* sank a freighter of 11,629 tonnes (11,446 tons), her largest victim so far, and on the night of 1/2 November she sank the Italian freighters *Balilla* and *Marigola* in gunfire engagements on the surface. On the night of 21/22 November *Utmost* torpedoed the Italian heavy cruiser *Trieste*, which managed to reach Messina with great difficulty.

In 1942, after refitting, *Utmost* received a new captain, Lt Coombe, and in November that year she sank after being damaged by depth-charges from the Italian torpedo boat *Ardente*. In that month Allied forces carried out a successful invasion of North Africa, and from then on the Axis forces were under pressure from two sides.

The contribution made to the eventual Allied victory by Malta-based submarines like *Utmost*, which preyed on the enemy's supply lines, was massive.

SPECIFICATIONS

UTMOST

Displacement surfaced: **554tnes (545t)**	Performance surfaced: **11.25 knots**
Displacement submerged: **752tnes (740t)**	Performance submerged: **9 knots**
Machinery: **two screws, diesel/electric motors; 825/615hp**	Armament: **four 533mm (21in) TT; one 76mm (3in) gun**
Length: **54.9m (180ft)**	Surface range: **7041km (3800nm)**
Beam: **4.8m (16ft)**	Crew: **31**
Draught: **3.8m (12ft 9in)**	Launch date: **20 April 1940**

X-CRAFT

SPECIFICATIONS

X-CRAFT

Displacement surfaced: **27tnes (25.4t)**	Performance surfaced: **6.5 knots**
Displacement submerged: **30tnes (29.5t)**	Performance submerged: **5 knots**
Machinery: **single screw, diesel/electric motors; 42/30hp**	Armament: **Explosive charges**
Length: **15.7m (51ft 6in)**	Surface range: **Not recorded**
Beam: **1.8m (6ft)**	Crew: **4**
Draught: **2.6m (8ft 6in)**	Launch date: **1942**

The Royal Navy's midget submarines of World War II, known as X-craft, had their origins in a small river submarine that was being developed for the British Army by a Commander Varley in 1939.

Two prototype X-craft, the *X3* and *X4*, were built by Varley Marine, while other X and XT boats (the latter intended for training only) were produced by Vickers. Another version, designated XE, was roomier than the others and was intended for use against the Japanese in the Far East.

The X and XE craft carried side charges, each containing about two tonnes (two tons) of explosives. Designed to be placed under the bottom of the target vessel, these explosives were activated by clockwork time fuses.

The X-craft carried out some notable wartime operations, including an attack on the German battleship *Tirpitz* in Kaafjord on 23 September 1943, causing damage that effectively prevented the warship from mounting offensive operations.

In the Far East, two X-craft, *XE-1* and *XE-3*, were used to make an effective attack on the Japanese cruiser *Takao* in Singapore harbour on 30 July 1945. The warship was damaged so badly that she sank to the bottom.

ADUA

The Italian submarine *Adua* was leader of a class of 17 short-range submarines completed for the Italian Navy between 1936 and 1937, at a time when Italy and France were striving to establish naval supremacy in the Mediterranean. In fact, these two nations built more submarines in the inter-war years than any other country.

The Adua-class boats were repeats of the previous Perla class. Although not endowed with a fast surface speed, they were highly manoeuvrable and structurally strong – both considerable advantages when taking evasive action.

All of the Adua-class boats gave excellent service during World War II, although only one, the *Alagi*, survived the conflict. The rest were either destroyed in engagements with British warships or sunk by bombing.

Adua herself was sunk in the western Mediterranean (off Algeria) in a depth charge attack by the HM destroyers *Gurkha* and *Legion* on 30 September 1941.

One of the problems with the design of the Adua-class submarines was that their conning towers were too large, making them readily visible when surfaced; as a result, small conning towers were fitted to some boats during the course of the war.

Two boats, *Gondar* and *Scire*, were equipped to carry human torpedoes.

SPECIFICATIONS

ADUA

Displacement surfaced: **691tnes (680t)**	*Performance surfaced:* **14 knots**
Displacement submerged: **880tnes (866t)**	*Performance submerged:* **7 knots**
Machinery: **two shaft, diesel/electric motors; 1200/800hp**	*Armament:* **eight 533mm (21in) TT; one 100mm (3.9in) gun**
Length: **60.2m (197ft 6in)**	*Surface range:* **18,530km (10,000nm) at 10 knots**
Beam: **6.5m (21ft 4in)**	*Crew:* **58**
Draught: **4.6mm (15ft)**	*Launch date:* **3 April 1938**

BRIN

SPECIFICATIONS

BRIN

Displacement surfaced:
1032tnes (1016t)

Performance surfaced:
17 knots

Displacement submerged:
1286tnes (1266t)

Performance submerged:
8 knots

Machinery:
**two screws,
diesel/electric motors;
3400/1300hp**

Armament:
**eight 533mm (21in)
TT; one 100mm
(3.9in) gun**

Length:
70m (231ft 4in)

Surface range:
**18,530km (10,000nm)
at 10 knots**

Beam:
7m (22ft 6in)

Crew:
58

Draught:
4.2m (13ft 6in)

Launch date:
3 April 1938

Derived from the Archimede class, the five Brin-class submarines were long-range boats, all launched between 1938 and 1939. Two of the boats were built in great secrecy and given the names *Archimede* and *Torricelli* to disguise the fact that two Archimede-class boats of the same name had earlier been transferred to Nationalist Spain.

Brin, named after the famous Italian naval engineer Benedetto Brin, was assigned to a submarine flotilla covering the approaches to the Aegean Sea just before Italy's entry into the war in June 1940, and in 1941 she deployed to the French Atlantic ports to take part in the Axis submarine offensive against the British Atlantic convoys. (At this period in the war, there were actually more Italian submarines than German ones operating in the Atlantic Ocean.)

After further operations in the Mediterranean, *Brin* was taken over by the Allies following the Italian armistice in September 1943 and transferred to the Royal Navy's Eastern Fleet, where she was used for anti-submarine warfare training in the Indian Ocean, though seeing no actual combat.

After performing a great deal of useful service under the Royal Navy, *Brin* was retired at the end of the war and discarded in 1948.

BARBARIGO

Completed in September 1938, *Barbarigo* was a Marcello-class submarine. She enjoyed a somewhat longer operational life than the majority of her 10 sister boats, most of which had been sunk by the end of 1942.

    Barbarigo, under Cdr Ghilieri, deployed to Bordeaux in the late summer of 1940 for operations in the Central Atlantic, which began in October. The boat had no success, apart from damaging a small freighter in a surface engagement, and in January 1942 she sank a neutral Spanish ship, the *Navemar*, which was returning empty after taking Jewish refugees from Cadiz to New York.

    On 6 October 1942, now under Cdr Grossi, she added farce to her record when she attacked the British corvette *Petunia*, which she mistook for an American battleship, and then claimed to have sunk her, mistaking depth-charge explosions for torpedo detonations.

    A new skipper, Lt-Cdr Rigoli, finally brought a measure of success to the boat, sinking three ships on the night of 8/9 March 1943. *Barbarigo* was subsequently converted as a supply submarine for service on the France-Japan route, but was sunk by Allied aircraft in the Bay of Biscay at the start of her first trip out in June 1943.

SPECIFICATIONS

BARBARIGO

Displacement surfaced: **1059tnes (1043t)**	Performance surfaced: **17.4 knots**
Displacement submerged: **1310tnes (1290t)**	Performance submerged: **8 knots**
Machinery: **twin screws, diesel/electric motors; 3600/1100hp**	Armament: **eight 533mm (21in) TT**
Length: **73m (239ft 6in)**	Surface range: **1425km (768nm) at 10 knots**
Beam: **7m (23ft)**	Crew: **58**
Draught: **5m (16ft 6in)**	Launch date: **13 June 1938**

CAGNI

SPECIFICATIONS

CAGNI

Displacement surfaced: **1528tnes (1504t)**	Performance surfaced: **17 knots**
Displacement submerged: **1707tnes (1680t)**	Performance submerged: **9 knots**
Machinery: **twin screws, diesel/electric motors; 4370/1800hp**	Armament: **14 450mm (17.7in) TT; two 100mm (3.9in) guns**
Length: **87.9m (200ft 5in)**	Surface range: **22,236km (12,000nm) at 11 knots**
Beam: **7.76m (17ft 7in)**	Crew: **85**
Draught: **5.72m (13ft)**	Launch date: **20 July 1940**

Endowed with an exceptionally long range, the four boats of the Ammiraglio Cagni class were the biggest attack submarines ever built for the Italian Navy. They were developed specifically for commerce raiding in distant waters, and carried a large number of lesser calibre 450mm (17.7in) torpedoes for use against unarmoured merchant ships.

However, *Cagni*'s first war mission, together with her sister boat *Ammiraglio Saint-Bon*, was to transport some 305 tonnes (300 tons) of fuel and supplies from Taranto to Bardia in October 1941 in support of the Axis war effort in North Africa, evading several air attacks en route. In November 1942, under Cdr Liannazza, *Cagni* emerged from the Mediterranean, sinking one ship en route and another when she reached her war station in the South Atlantic. This first patrol lasted no less than four and a half months, an indication of *Cagni*'s excellent endurance.

During another long patrol, this time under the command of Cdr Rosselli-Lorenzini, she torpedoed the British auxiliary cruiser *Asturias* on 25 July 1943, but had no further success before the Italian surrender in September, after which she sailed into Durban.

She was the only survivor of the four boats, and was scrapped in 1948.

CALVI

One of three ocean-going boats in her class, *Pietro Calvi* was completed in October 1935. She was one of the first Italian boats to deploy to the recently captured Atlantic ports in the summer of 1940 following the fall of France, and under Cdr Caridi sank her first merchant ship in December.

A year later, having proved spectacularly unsuccessful on further Atlantic patrols, and having received a new captain, Cdr Olivieri, she was involved in a major rescue mission to pick up two sets of survivors, those of the German U-boat supply ship *Python*, which had been sunk by the British cruiser *Dorsetshire*, and those of the commerce raider *Atlantis*, sunk by the British cruiser *Devonshire*.

The rescue operation was extremely hazardous because the crews of the sunken ships had to be towed on floats by German submarines, already crammed with survivors, until the larger Italian boats could come up and take the remainder on board.

Olivieri proved to be a skilled captain. Between 25 March and 12 April 1942 he sank five ships off the coast of Brazil. On 15 July 1942, however, *Calvi* was forced to the surface while attempting to attack a convoy and sunk after a violent gun battle with British escort vessels, most notably HMS *Lulworth*.

SPECIFICATIONS

CALVI

Displacement surfaced: **1574tnes (1500t)**	Performance surfaced: **17 knots**
Displacement submerged: **2092tnes (2060t)**	Performance submerged: **8 knots**
Machinery: **twin screws, diesel/electric motors; 4400/1800**	Armament: **eight 533mm (21in) TT; two 120mm (4.7in) guns**
Length: **84.3m (276ft 6in)**	Surface range: **19,311km (10,409nm) at 10 knots**
Beam: **7.7m (25ft 3in)**	Crew: **77**
Draught: **5.2m (17ft)**	Launch date: **31 March 1935**

DANDOLO

SPECIFICATIONS

DANDOLO

Displacement surfaced:
1080tnes (1063t)

Performance surfaced:
17.4 knots

Displacement submerged:
1338tnes (1317t)

Performance submerged:
8 knots

Machinery:
two screws,
diesel/electric motors;
2880/1250hp

Armament:
eight 533mm (21in)
TT; two 100mm
(3.9in) guns

Length:
73m (239ft 6in)

Surface range:
4750km (2560nm)
at 17 knots

Beam:
7.2m (23ft 8in)

Crew:
57

Draught:
5m (16ft 5in)

Launch date:
20 November 1937

A sister vessel to *Barbarigo*, *Dandolo* was one of the nine ocean-going boats of the Marcello class, designed by the talented engineer Curio Bernardis. Her first war patrol in June 1940 was unlucky, her torpedoes just missing the new French cruiser *Jean de Vienne*.

After initial operations in the Atlantic off Madeira and the Azores, *Dandolo* (Cdr Boris) and other Italian submarines deployed to Bordeaux, from where they operated against Allied commerce in the Central Atlantic. *Dandolo* enjoyed some success, sinking one freighter of 5270 tonnes (5187 tons) and damaging another of 3828 tonnes (3768 tons). She continued to operate from Bordeaux during the winter of 1940-41, subsequently returning to Italy for a refit before recommencing operations.

Under the command of Lt-Cdr Auconi *Dandolo* sank a number of merchant ships, then acted in the role of transport submarine for a time before returning to offensive operations. On 20 July 1942, she fired a salvo of four torpedoes, all of which missed, at the aircraft carrier HMS *Eagle*. In July 1940, during the Allied invasion of Sicily, she torpedoed and damaged the British cruiser *Cleopatra*. She survived the war and was discarded in 1947.

FOCA

Completed in November 1937, *Foca* was one of three minelaying submarines, the other two being *Atropo* and *Zoea*. They were the last of such boats to be built for the Italian Navy before World War II.

On these boats the torpedo armament was sacrificed to provide two mine chutes at the stern. As originally configured, the 100mm (3.9in) gun was mounted in a shielded position in the after section of the conning tower, but this was later replaced by a gun mounted on the casing forward of the conning tower.

Foca was an early war loss; in October 1940 she sailed to lay a mine barrage off the coast of Palestine near Haifa and never returned. The theory was that she had run into a British minefield. Her two sister boats both survived the war, having surrendered at the time of the armistice in September 1943.

In November, *Atropo* and *Zoea*, together with the *Corridoni* and *Menotti*, joined the British boats *Severn* and *Rorqual* in transporting some 305 tonnes (300 tons) of supplies to the Aegean islands of Leros and Samos, which had been seized and occupied by British commandos. The Germans reacted swiftly and regained control of the islands, most of the British garrisons being captured after a fierce fight. *Atropo* and *Zoea* were both discarded in March 1947.

SPECIFICATIONS

FOCA

Displacement surfaced:
1354tnes (1333t)

Displacement submerged:
1685tnes (1659t)

Machinery:
twin screws, diesel/electric motors; 2880/1250hp

Length:
82.8m (271ft 8in)

Beam:
7.2m (23ft 6in)

Draught:
5.3m (17ft 5in)

Performance surfaced:
15.2 knots

Performance submerged:
7.4 knots

Armament:
six 533mm (21in) TT; one 100mm (3.9in) gun

Surface range:
4632nm (2500nm) at 17 knots

Crew:
60

Launch date:
26 June 1937

FLUTTO

SPECIFICATIONS

FLUTTO

Displacement surfaced: **973tnes (958t)**	Performance surfaced: **16 knots**
Displacement submerged: **1189tnes (1170t)**	Performance submerged: **7 knots**
Machinery: **twin screws, diesel/electric motors**	Armament: **six 533mm (21in) TT**
Length: **63.2m (207ft)**	Surface range: **5297km (3200nm)**
Beam: **7m (23ft)**	Crew: **50**
Draught: **4.9m (16ft)**	Launch date: **November 1942**

The *Flutto* was the class leader of the first of three planned groups of submarines that would have reached a total of 49 boats, all embodying the lessons absorbed by the Italian Navy since it entered the war in June 1940. The plan called for production to be completed by the end of 1944; in the event, production was overtaken by the armistice of September 1943, and only a few of the first group, including class leader *Flutto*, ever saw active military service.

Two of the class, *Grongo* and *Murena*, were fitted with cylinders for transporting human torpedoes. *Flutto* was sunk by Royal Navy MTBs *640, 651* and *670* in the Straits of Messina on 11 July 1943, during the Allied invasion of Sicily, Operation Husky.

Of her sister boats, *Gorgo* was sunk by the American destroyer USS *Nields* off Algeria on 21 May 1943, and *Tritone* was sunk by gunfire from the British destroyer *Antelope* and the Canadian corvette *Port Arthur* off Bougie on 19 January 1943.

Other boats in the class were sunk in harbour after being seized by the Germans or destroyed in various stages of construction by Allied air attacks. One, the *Nautilo*, was refloated and handed over to the Yugoslav Navy as the *Sava*; the *Murea* went to the USSR in 1949, designated the *Z13*.

GALILEI

Assigned to the Nationalist forces during the Spanish Civil War, the Archimede-class submarine *Galileo Galilei* gave the Italian Navy much valuable experience of operational patrolling in a war zone, an experience shared by her sister boat, *Galileo Ferraris*.

The class leader, *Archimede*, was secretly transferred to Spain in 1937, together with the *Evangelista Torricelli*, the boats being respectively named *General Sanjurjo* and *General Mola*.

Italy's entry into the war on the Axis side in June 1940 found *Galilei* and *Ferraris* at their war stations in the Red Sea, *Ferraris* making an unsuccessful attempt to attack the British battleship *Royal Sovereign*, which was passing through the Suez Canal.

On 10 October, *Galilei* engaged the British armed trawler *Moonstone*, whose accurate gunfire killed nearly all the submarine's officers and damaged the air-conditioning system, which emitted toxic fumes and asphyxiated those crew members inside the boat. Floating on the sea, *Galilei* was taken into Royal Navy service as training boat *X2*, with the pennant number *P.711*. She was discarded in 1946.

Her sister boat *Ferraris* was caught on the surface and sunk by air attack and gunfire in the North Atlantic on 25 October 1941.

SPECIFICATIONS

GALILEI

Displacement surfaced: **1000tnes (985t)**	*Performance surfaced:* **17 knots**
Displacement submerged: **1279tnes (1259t)**	*Performance submerged:* **8.5 knots**
Machinery: **twin screws, diesel/electric motors; 3000/1300hp**	*Armament:* **eight 533mm (21in) TT; two 100mm (3.9in) guns**
Length: **70.5m (231ft 4in)**	*Surface range:* **6670km (3600nm)**
Beam: **6.8m (22ft 4in)**	*Crew:* **55**
Draught: **4m (13ft 5in)**	*Launch date:* **19 March 1934**

MAMELI

SPECIFICATIONS

MAMELI

Displacement surfaced:
  843tnes (830t)

Performance surfaced:
  17 knots

Displacement submerged:
  1026tnes (1010t)

Performance submerged:
  7 knots

Machinery:
  twin screws,
  diesel/electric motors;
  3000/1100hp

Armament:
  six 533mm (21in)
  TT; one 102mm
  (4in) gun

Length:
  64.6m (212ft)

Surface range:
  5930km (3200nm)
  at 10 knots

Beam:
  6.5m (21ft 4in)

Crew:
  49

Draught:
  4.3m (14ft)

Launch date:
  9 December 1926

The four Mameli-class submarines were, in effect, prototypes for several of the Italian Navy's subsequent ocean-going submarine designs, and were the first of their type to come into service after World War I, during which Italy had fought Germany.

The design of the Mameli-class boats incorporated much that had been learned from an appraisal of captured German U-boats, and the Mameli class were able to reach diving depths that had not previously been possible with Italian boats.

Goffredo Mameli (previously named *Masaniello*) and two of her sister boats, *Giovanni Procida* and *Tito Speri*, all survived World War II and were discarded in 1948. The fourth boat, *Pier Capponi*, was torpedoed by HM submarine *Rorqual* south of Stromboli on 31 March 1941.

All four submarines saw active service in support of Nationalist forces during the Spanish Civil War. *Mameli*, under Cdr Maiorana, had an early success in the weeks after Italy entered the war, sinking a freighter between Alexandria and Crete, but apart from that she had a particularly undistinguished war. As with other Italian submarines of this period, the large surface area of her conning tower proved an excellent target and hence a disadvantage.

PERLA

One of 10 submarines in her class, all completed in 1936, *Perla* was on patrol in the Indian Ocean when Italy entered the war. Under Lt-Cdr Napp, she remained there until early March 1941, when she departed Massawa and sailed for Bordeaux via the Cape of Good Hope, being replenished en route by the German commerce raider *Atlantis*. With *Perla* went the other Italian submarines *Archimede*, *Guglielmotti* and *Ferraris*.

By the spring of 1942 *Perla* was back in the Mediterranean, attacking Royal Navy Malta convoys and seeking targets in the waters around Cyprus. This part of the eastern Mediterranean was rich in oil-tanker traffic, which regularly plied its trade between Syrian ports and Egypt.

It was while carrying out these activities, on 9 July 1942, that *Perla* was forced to the surface and captured off Beirut by the British corvette *Hyacinth*.

She was eventually handed over to the Royal Hellenic Navy and renamed *Matrozos*, serving on patrol duty around the islands in the Aegean until the end of World War II. She was scrapped in 1954.

Two of the Perla-class boats, *Iride* and *Ambra*, were fitted with canisters for the carriage of human torpedoes. Five of this class were lost by the Italian Navy during World War II.

SPECIFICATIONS

PERLA

Displacement surfaced: **707tnes (696t)**	Performance surfaced: **14 knots**
Displacement submerged: **865tnes (852t)**	Performance submerged: **8 knots**
Machinery: **two screws, diesel/electric motors; 1400/800hp**	Armament: **six 533mm (21in) TT; one 100mm (3.9in) gun**
Length: **60m (196ft 9in)**	Surface range: **6670km (3595nm) at 10 knots**
Beam: **6.5m (21ft 2in)**	Crew: **45**
Draught: **5m (15ft 3in)**	Launch date: **3 May 1936**

SQUALO

SPECIFICATIONS

SQUALO

Displacement surfaced: **948tnes (933t)**	Performance surfaced: **15 knots**
Displacement submerged: **1160tnes (1142t)**	Performance submerged: **8 knots**
Machinery: **two diesel/ electric motors; 3000/1300hp**	Armament: **eight 533mm (21in) TT; one 102mm (4in) gun**
Length: **70m (229ft)**	Surface range: **7412km (4000nm) at 10 knots**
Beam: **7m (23ft 7in)**	Crew: **52**
Draught: **7m (23ft 7in)**	Launch date: **15 January 1930**

The leader of a class of four submarines, *Squalo* was on patrol in the eastern Mediterranean when Italy declared war on the Allies, covering an area from the Aegean to the Levant.

Apart from accounting for a few small sailing craft, sunk by gunfire on the surface (nearly all World War II submarines, of whatever navy, were designed to attack their targets on the surface), her operations were unsuccessful; this was mainly due to the fact that Italian naval intelligence on the movements of British shipping was almost always defective, and submarines were ordered to patrol the wrong areas.

Other Squalo-class boats, however, enjoyed more success. On July 1941, for example, *Delfino* shot down the RAF *Sunderland* flying boat that was attacking her and took four of its crew prisoner. Such instances were comparatively rare, but not unknown during air-sea warfare in World War II.

Delfino was accidentally sunk in a collision in 1943. Of the other two boats, *Narvalo* was scuttled after being damaged by British destroyers off Tripoli in January 1943, while *Tricheco* was sunk by HM submarine *Upholder* off Brindisi in March 1942.

Squalo was discarded in 1948, having been laid up before Italy's armistice with the Allies.

I-7

The J3 class submarine *I-7* and her sister boat, *I-8*, were among the first submarines of pure Japanese design and, at the time of their commissioning, were the largest in the Imperial Japanese Navy. They would begin a trend for large submarines in the Japanese Navy, a trend that was to prove utterly futile in serving Japan's wartime needs. Large submarines used lots of fuel and had short endurance at sea.

Approved in the 1934 naval construction programme, their design was based on a submarine cruiser concept, developed from the earlier KD3 and KD4 designs, and they had provision for a Yokosuka E14Y1 reconnaissance seaplane (codenamed Glen by the Allies).

The aircraft made its operational debut on 17 December 1941, when *I-7* launched its Glen on a dawn reconnaissance over Pearl Harbor to assess the damage done by carrier-based attack aircraft. *I-7* had an endurance of 60 days and a respectable diving depth of 99m (325ft).

I-7 and her sister sank seven Allied merchant vessels, totalling 42,574 tonnes (41,902 tons) during the course of the Pacific war. *I-7* was sunk by the American destroyer *Monaghan* off the Aleutian islands on 22 June 1943, while *I-8* was sunk by the destroyers USS *Morrison* and *Stockton* off Okinawa on 30 March 1945.

SPECIFICATIONS

I-7

Displacement surfaced: **2565tnes (2525t)**	Performance surfaced: **23 knots**
Displacement submerged: **3640tnes (3583t)**	Performance submerged: **8 knots**
Machinery: **twin screws, diesel/electric motors; 11,200/2800hp**	Armament: **six 533mm (21in) TT; one 140mm (5.5in) gun**
Length: **109.3m (358ft 7in)**	Surface range: **26,600km (14,337nm) at 16 knots**
Beam: **9m (29ft 6in)**	Crew: **100**
Draught: **5.2m (17ft)**	Launch date: **3 July 1935**

I-15

SPECIFICATIONS

I-15

Displacement surfaced:
2625tnes (2584t)

Displacement submerged:
3713tnes (3654t)

Machinery:
two screws,
diesel/electric motors;
12,400/2000hp

Length:
102.5m (336ft)

Beam:
9.3m (30ft 6in)

Draught:
5.1m (16ft 9in)

Performance surfaced:
23.5 knots

Performance submerged:
8 knots

Armament:
six 533mm (21in) TT;
one 140mm (5.5in) and
two 25mm AA guns

Surface range:
29,648km (16,000nm)

Crew:
100

Launch date:
7 March 1939

Developed from the earlier KD6-class cruiser-type submarines, the I-15 class were designed for long-range scouting. Like the I-7 class, they were equipped with a Yokosuka E14Y1 Glen reconnaissance seaplane, which on one occasion was used as a bomber aircraft.

In 1942, a Glen flown by Warrant Officer Fujita was launched from the I-15-class submarine *I-25*, which was cruising off the US west coast. The aircraft carried four 76kg (168lb) incendiary bombs in place of its observer, and these were dropped in a forested area of Oregon, causing limited damage. It was the first and only time that the continental United States was attacked by an enemy aircraft.

The I-15-class boats saw extensive war service, one of their missions being to run supplies and diplomatic personnel to and from Japan and the French Atlantic ports. On 15 October 1942 *I-15* and her sister boat *I-19* took part in a highly successful attack on the aircraft carrier USS *Wasp*, which was hit by *I-19* and had to be abandoned, and the destroyer *O'Brien*, which was torpedoed by *I-15* and sank four days later.

On 27 October *I-15* narrowly missed the battleship *Washington*. The submarine was herself sunk on 2 November 1942.

I-16

Ordered in 1937, the five boats of the I-16 class were the first Japanese submarines to be laid down in the scramble for naval expansion that followed the expiry of the London Naval Treaty.

Optimized for attack, they carried a heavy armament and had an endurance of 90 days. Prior to the attack on Pearl Harbor the five submarines (*I-16*, *I-18*, *I-20*, *I-22* and *I-24*) each loaded a Type A midget submarine on a fitting abaft the conning tower and launched them off the US naval base on the night of 6/7 December 1941. All the midgets were unsuccessful, however.

One of the midget craft was sunk by the destroyer USS *Ward* in the first action of the Pacific War, two were sunk penetrating the harbour and the other two in the harbour itself before they could launch their torpedoes at their targets.

At the beginning of 1943, *I-16* was modified as a transport submarine, with provision for a Daihatsu landing craft and other equipment for supplying Japanese troops on beleaguered islands. On 14 May 1944, while on just such a transport mission to the Solomons, *I-16* was located by a US destroyer escort group and sunk by a "hedgehog" salvo.

The other four boats were also sunk during the war, all between 1942 and 1943.

SPECIFICATIONS

I-16

Displacement surfaced: **2595tnes (2554t)**	*Performance surfaced:* **23.6 knots**
Displacement submerged: **3618tnes (3561t)**	*Performance submerged:* **8 knots**
Machinery: **two screws, diesel/electric motors; 12,400/2000hp**	*Armament:* **eight 533mm (21in) TT; one 140mm (5.5in) and two 25mm AA guns**
Length: **103.80m (340ft 7in)**	*Surface range:* **25,942km (14,000nm)**
Beam: **9.10m (29ft 10in)**	*Crew:* **100**
Draught: **5.35m (17ft 7in)**	*Launch date:* **28 July 1938**

I-52

SPECIFICATIONS

I-52

Displacement surfaced: **2605tnes (2564t)**	Performance surfaced: **17.7 knots**
Displacement submerged: **3618tnes (3561t)**	Performance submerged: **6.5 knots**
Machinery: **two screws, diesel/electric motors; 4700/1200hp**	Armament: **six 533mm (21in) TT; two 140mm (5.5in) and two 25mm AA guns**
Length: **102.4m (335ft 11in)**	Surface range: **38,913km (21,000nm) at 16 knots**
Beam: **9.3m (30ft 6in)**	Crew: **101**
Draught: **5.12m (16ft 10in)**	Launch date: **1943**

The five I-52 class (Type C3) submarines were authorized in 1942 under the Japanese 1941–42 War Programme, but only three were built.

The I-52 class submarines were generally similar to those of the preceding I-16 (C2) class, except that they carried a reduced number of torpedoes and less powerful diesel engines, the higher-powered units at that time being in short supply. The reduction in weight and increase in space meant that extra fuel could be carried, greatly enhancing the operational radius of these boats. However, even with greater range these vessels were still vulnerable to roving Allied aircraft.

I-52 herself was modified as a transport submarine, embarking on her first voyage to Europe via the Indian Ocean in May 1944. On the night of 23/24 June, having made rendezvous with the German *U-530* to take on board specialist search radar equipment, she was sunk near the Azores by Grumman Avenger aircraft from the carrier USS *Bogue*, the Avengers fixing her position with the help of sonobuoys, recently developed in the United States of America.

Of the other two boats, *I-53* was converted to a Kaiten midget submarine carrier and survived the war, being scuttled by the United States Navy in 1946, while *I-55* was sunk by US forces off Tinian on 28 July 1944.

I-58

The *I-58* was one of three Type B3 submarines that were completed between March and September 1944. *I-56* and *I-58* were converted to Kaiten midget submarine carriers, and in January 1945, together with other similarly equipped submarines, they took part in Operation Kongo, in which attempted attacks were made on US naval bases.

The missions by *I-56* and *I-58*, against Manus in the Admiralty Islands and by *I-58* on Apra Harbour on Guam, were unsuccessful. Similar operations in opposition to the American landings on the island of Iwo Jima also proved abortive, but on the night of 27/28 July the submarine, under Cdr Hashimoto, launched a Kaiten and probably damaged the destroyer USS *Lowry*.

The action that assured *I-58* a place in naval history, however, occurred on the night of 29/30 July, when she launched a salvo of six torpedoes at the unescorted heavy cruiser USS *Indianapolis* (Capt McVay) east of Luzon. The cruiser was making for Leyte at speed after delivering parts of atomic bombs from San Francisco to Tinian, from where the fateful missions against Hiroshima and Nagasaki were flown. Of the cruiser's crew of 1199 only 316 survived. *I-58* was scuttled by the US Navy in April 1946.

SPECIFICATIONS

I-58

Displacement surfaced: **2605tnes (2564t)**	*Performance surfaced:* **17.7 knots**
Displacement submerged: **3618tnes (3561t)**	*Performance submerged:* **6.5 knots**
Machinery: **two screws, diesel/electric motors; 4700/1200hp**	*Armament:* **six 533mm (21in) TT; two 140mm (5.5in) and two 25mm AA guns**
Length: **102.40m (335ft 11in)**	*Surface range:* **38,913km (21,000nm) at 16 knots**
Beam: **9.30m (30ft 6in)**	*Crew:* **101**
Draught: **5.12m (16ft 10in)**	*Launch date:* **1944**

KAITEN

SPECIFICATIONS

KAITEN

Displacement surfaced: **unknown**	Performance surfaced: **30 knots maximum**
Displacement submerged: **8.6tnes (8.5t)**	Performance submerged: **unknown**
Machinery: **one 550hp petrol-oxygen engine**	Armament: **one 1550kg (3416lb) HE warhead**
Length: **14.73m (48ft)**	Surface range: **92km (50nm) at 12 knots/25km (14nm) at 30 knots**
Beam: **0.99m (3ft 4in)**	Crew: **1**
Draught: **3.61m (3ft 3in)**	Launch date: **1944–45**

The Kaiten midget submarines, deployed in the closing months of World War II, were the Imperial Japanese Navy's equivalent of the Kamikaze suicide aircraft. They were built onto the body of a Type 93 torpedo engine and air chamber, and early models were provided with a small hatch under the hull to enable the pilot to escape as soon as the craft was locked on to its target. This escape facility was later removed, and the Kaiten became a true suicide weapon.

The *Kaiten 1* was powered by petrol and oxygen. The next version, the *Kaiten 2*, was powered by a hydrogen peroxide engine, but only a few examples were built as insufficient engines of this type were available. As a consequence, a *Kaiten 4* was built, using the conventional petrol and oxygen engine and carrying a heavier warhead to ensure penetration of enemy hulls.

The *Kaiten 3* was an experimental unit which never entered production. The *Kaiten 2* and *4* carried a two-man crew. Hundreds of Kaiten were built, and were intended to be used primarily for coastal defence in opposition to the expected invasion of Japan, although many were deployed against Allied naval forces elsewhere and were first used in the battle for the Philippines, November 1944. The specifications table at left is for the *Kaiten 1*.

I-121

The four I-121-class (Type KRS) submarines were developed from the former German *U-125*, which had been surrendered to Japan after World War I, and were virtually identical in performance, size and appearance. All four were intended specifically for minelaying, and could carry 42 mines in addition to their complement of torpedoes.

On the night of 6/7 December 1941, just prior to the attack on Pearl Harbor, *I-121* (Cdr Yendo) and *I-122* (Cdr Utsuki) laid mine barrages off the north-east exits from Singapore. The same two boats sowed more mines off Singapore between 8 and 15 December, while their sister submarines *I-123* (Cdr Ueno) and *I-124* (Cdr Kishigami) carried out similar operations off the Philippines, the latter boat also sinking a ship with her four torpedoes.

Later in December all four boats were involved in minelaying in Indonesian waters, and in January 1942 they were in Australian waters, *I-124* being sunk off Port Darwin on the 20th.

In the summer of 1942 the remaining boats acted as tankers for fleet reconnaissance aircraft off the Hawaiian Islands. During the battle off the Solomon Islands in August, *I-121* was damaged by carrier aircraft and later relegated to the training role. She was scrapped in 1946.

SPECIFICATIONS

I-121

Displacement surfaced: **1405tnes (1383t)**	Performance surfaced: **14.5 knots**
Displacement submerged: **1796tnes (1768t)**	Performance submerged: **7 knots**
Machinery: **two screws, diesel/electric motors; 2400/1100hp**	Armament: **four 533mm (21in) TT; one 140mm (5.5in) gun, two mines**
Length: **82m (269ft)**	Surface range: **19,456km (10,500nm) at 8 knots**
Beam: **7.52m (24ft 8in)**	Crew: **75**
Draught: **4.42m (14ft 6in)**	Launch date: **unknown**

I-153

SPECIFICATIONS

I-153

Displacement surfaced:
1828tnes (1800t)

Displacement submerged:
2337tnes (2300t)

Machinery:
**two screws,
diesel/electric motors;
6800/1800hp**

Length:
94.49m (310ft)

Beam:
7.98m (26ft 2in)

Draught:
4.83m (15ft 10in)

Performance surfaced:
20 knots

Performance submerged:
8 knots

Armament:
**eight 533mm (21in) TT;
one 105mm (4.7in) gun**

Surface range:
**18,530km (10,000nm)
at 8 knots**

Crew:
60

Launch date:
5 August 1925

The *I-153* was one of four Type KD3a boats approved in the extensive 1923–28 Japanese naval building programme and completed between March and December 1927.

Originally designated *No 64*, she later became *I-53*; two other boats were designated *No 77* (*I-54*) and *No 78* (*I-55*) respectively. The fourth boat, *I-58*, did not have a prior number and is sometimes classed as a Type KD3b.

All the surviving boats were renumbered in May 1942, *I-53* becoming *I-153* and so on. Before that, *I-53* was active in the waters around the Dutch East Indies archipelago, attacking ships evacuating Allied personnel from Java. During these operations, *I-53*, under Cdr Nakamura, sank three ships totalling 11,178 tonnes (11,002 tons).

During the Pacific war, submarines of the KD3a and KD3b classes, nine boats in all, sank 17 Allied ships totalling 63,380 tonnes (62,379 tons). By the summer of 1942 all submarines in this class had been relegated to the training role, although some were later reinstated as Kaiten carriers.

I-153 and *I-154* were disarmed in 1944 and surrendered at the end of the war, being scrapped by the Americans in 1946.

I-201

The I-201 class of very advanced submarines owed its origin to an experimental submarine from 1937, known as *No 71*. Endowed with a very streamlined hull, *No 71* attained a remarkably high underwater speed of 21.75 knots, even though on average her electric motors produced only 1800hp.

No 71 was scrapped in 1940, after she had been exhaustively tested, and much of the data she yielded was incorporated in the *I-201* and her sister boats, ordered under an emergency war construction programme between 1943 and 1944, when Japan was losing heavily.

The *I-201* compared very favourably with the German Type XXI and in fact used lightweight MAN diesels of German origin, coupled with 5000hp electric motors that gave an impressive underwater speed of 19 knots, which could be maintained for nearly an hour. The boats had an endurance of 25 days and had a diving depth of 108m (355ft), deeper than any other Japanese submarine, but to no avail.

None of the I-201 (Type ST) class ever carried out a war patrol, most of the boats, including *I-201*, being scuttled by the US Navy after the end of the war. Only *I-204* was lost to enemy action, being sunk in an air attack at Kure on 22 June 1945 when almost complete and ready for sea.

SPECIFICATIONS

I-201

Displacement surfaced:
1311tnes (1291t)

Displacement submerged:
1473tnes (1450t)

Machinery:
**twin screws,
diesel/electric motors;
2750/5000hp**

Length:
79m (259ft 2in)

Beam:
5.8m (19ft)

Draught:
5.4m (17ft 9in)

Performance surfaced:
15.7 knots

Performance submerged:
19 knots

Armament:
**four 533mm (21in) TT;
two 25mm AA guns**

Surface range:
**10,747km (5800nm)
at 14 knots**

Crew:
100

Launch date:
1944

I-351

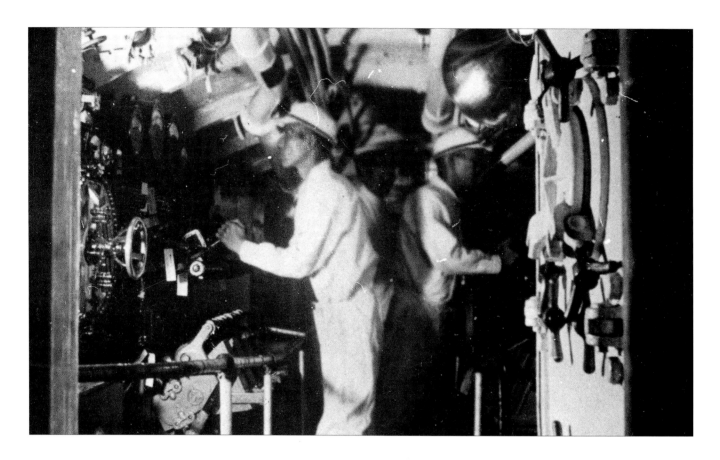

SPECIFICATIONS

I-351

Displacement surfaced:
3568tnes (3512t)

Displacement submerged:
4358tnes (4290t)

Machinery:
**twin screws,
diesel/electric motors**

Length:
110m (361ft)

Beam:
10.2m (33ft 6in)

Draught:
6m (20ft)

Performance surfaced:
15.7 knots

Performance submerged:
19 knots

Armament:
four 533mm (12in) TT

Surface range:
24,089km (13,000nm)

Crew:
90

Launch date:
1944

In 1941, the Japanese Admiralty foresaw that both flying boats and seaplanes would have a major part to play in a war that encompassed the vast expanse of the Pacific, particularly from the aerial reconnaissance point of view, and that these aircraft were not always likely to have the benefit of shore-based facilities – a basically sound theory.

A requirement was therefore formulated for a class of three submarines (Type SH) configured as mobile supply bases, equipped to carry 396 tonnes (390 tons) of cargo, including 371 tonnes (365 tons) of petrol, 11 tonnes (11 tons) of fresh water and 60 250kg (550lb) bombs, or alternatively 30 bombs and 15 aircraft torpedoes (the Germans used similar supply vessels).

Only one boat, the *I-351*, was completed and the third (*I-353*) was cancelled in 1943.

The *I-351*'s operational career was shortlived. On 14 July 1945 she was torpedoed and sunk by the American submarine USS *Bluefish* (Lt-Cdr Forbes) while operating in the area of Southeast Asia. The second boat, *I-352*, was 90 per cent complete when she was destroyed in an air attack on Kure.

The boats of this class had a safe diving depth of 96m (315ft) and had an underwater range of 185km (100nm) at three knots.

I-400

In 1942, at the instigation of Imperial Japanese Navy Commander-in-Chief Admiral Isoroku Yamamoto, the Navy Planning Staff investigated the feasibility of mounting a torpedo attack on the locks of the Panama Canal, using aircraft launched from a submarine.

Yamamoto pressed a reluctant Imperial HQ to go ahead with the building of 19 very large submarines capable of carrying two or three aircraft, and the result was the *I-400* Type STo.

In the event, only two submarines, *I-400* and *I-401*, were completed as aircraft carriers, being fitted with a large aircraft hangar offset to starboard. The hangar could accommodate three Aichi M6A1 Seiran floatplanes, plus components for a fourth. To launch the aircraft, the submarine would surface, then the machines would be warmed up in the hangar before being rolled out, their wings unfolded, and launched down a 26m (85ft) catapult rail.

The Panama mission, which was never a viable option for the Japanese Navy, was never flown, and the two boats were surrendered in 1945 and scrapped by the US Navy in 1946. Also scrapped by the USN was *I-402*, completed on the stocks as a submarine tanker/transport. Another boat, *I-404*, was almost complete when she was sunk at her moorings in an air raid.

SPECIFICATIONS

I-400

Displacement surfaced: 5316tnes (5233t)	**Performance surfaced:** 18.7 knots
Displacement submerged: 6665tnes (6560t)	**Performance submerged:** 6.5 knots
Machinery: twin screws, diesel/electric motors; 7700/2400hp	**Armament:** eight 533mm (21in) TT; one 140mm (5.5in) gun
Length: 116m (380ft 7in)	**Surface range:** 68,561km (37,000nm) at 14 knots
Beam: 12m (39ft 4in)	**Crew:** 100
Draught: 7m (23ft)	**Launch date:** 1944

RO-100

SPECIFICATIONS

RO-100

Displacement surfaced: **611tnes (601t)**	Performance surfaced: **14 knots**
Displacement submerged: **795tnes (782t)**	Performance submerged: **8 knots**
Machinery: **twin screws, diesel/electric motors; 1100/760hp**	Armament: **four 533mm (21in) TT; one 76mm (3in) gun**
Length: **57.4m (188ft 3in)**	Surface range: **6485km (3500nm) at 12 knots**
Beam: **6.1m (20ft)**	Crew: **75**
Draught: **3.5m (11ft 6in)**	Launch date: **6 December 1941**

Ordered under the Japanese Navy's 1940 and 1941 programmes, the 18 Ro-100 (Type KS) small, medium-class submarines were intended for use in coastal waters, within easy reach of their operational bases. Because of this they had an operational endurance of only three weeks. Submerged range was 111km (60nm) at 3 knots and they had a diving depth of 75m (245ft).

The class enjoyed some success during the Pacific war, sinking six merchant ships totalling 35,247 tonnes (34,690 tons) and damaging three more totalling 14,300 tonnes (14,074 tons). In addition, Ro-106 (Lt Nakamura) sank the tank landing ship *LST 342* off New Georgia on 18 July 1943, while *Ro-108* sank the US destroyer *Henley* off Finschhafen (New Guinea) on 3 October 1943.

All 18 boats became war losses. *Ro-100*'s operational career began in January 1943, when she operated in the area of the Solomons and off New Guinea. She was sunk on 25 November 1943 while carrying out a transport mission in support of operations in the New Hebrides.

Five other boats of the Ro-100 class were sunk in a period of only eight days in May 1944 by the escort destroyer USS *England*.

JASTRZAB

The *Jastrzab* (Hawk) was the former American submarine *S25*, which had been scheduled for delivery to the Royal Navy for trials to assess the possible usefulness of the older US S- and R-class boats by the British. Instead, for propaganda reasons, she was commissioned in 1941 as the Polish *Jastrzab*, flying the White Ensign of the RN as well as the flag of Poland and carrying the pennant number *P.551* (Poland had been overrun in 1939).

Jastrzab was manned by the crew of the Polish submarine *Wilk*. Despite the fact that all S-class boats assigned to the RN were relegated to training duties, *Jastrzab*'s crew insisted on being sent into action, and at the end of April 1942 she was deployed as part of the screening force for the Russian convoy PQ.15, a highly hazardous mission.

On 2 May, having departed from her assigned station, she was attacked and sunk in error by the Norwegian destroyer *St Albans* and the British minesweeper *Seagull* in the Norwegian Sea.

Jastrzab/*S25* was one of six S-class boats allocated to the Royal Navy. They were mostly used for training. Of the others, *P.553* and *P.554* were loaned to the Royal Canadian Navy, while *P.552* served in the Eastern Fleet and the South Atlantic.

SPECIFICATIONS

JASTRZAB

Displacement surfaced: **864tnes (850t)**	Performance surfaced: **14.5 knots**
Displacement submerged: **1107tnes (1090t)**	Performance submerged: **11 knots**
Machinery: **two screws, diesel/electric motors; 1200/1500hp**	Armament: **four 533mm (21in) TT; one 102mm (4in) gun**
Length: **64.3m (211ft)**	Surface range: **7782km (4200nm)**
Beam: **6.25m (20ft 6in)**	Crew: **42**
Draught: **4.6m (15ft 3in)**	Launch date: **29 May 1922**

ORZEL

SPECIFICATIONS

ORZEL

Displacement surfaced:
1117tnes (1100t)

Performance surfaced:
15 knots

Displacement submerged:
1496tnes (1473t)

Performance submerged:
8 knots

Machinery:
**twin screws,
diesel/electric motors;
4740/1100hp**

Armament:
**12 550mm (21.7in)
TT; one 105mm
(4in) gun**

Length:
84m (275ft 7in)

Surface range:
**13,300km (7169nm)
at 10 knots**

Beam:
6.7m (22ft)

Crew:
56

Draught:
4m (13ft 8in)

Launch date:
15 January 1938

Commissioned on 2 February 1939, the large ocean-going Polish submarine *Orzel* (Eagle) was built with funds raised by public subscription. She was built in Holland at De Schelde Navy Yard, Vlissingen; her sister boat, *Sep*, was built at Rotterdam Dockyard. The latter boat was still in Rotterdam in April 1939 and sailed for Gdynia before her builders' trials were completed in order to escape possible German sabotage following the invasion of Czechoslovakia.

Both boats put to sea when Germany attacked Poland at the beginning of September, *Sep* being interned at Stavnas, Sweden, on 17 September 1939; *Orzel* was likewise interned at Tallin on 15 September, some of her equipment being confiscated.

Despite the odds against him, *Orzel*'s commander, Lt-Cdr Grudzinski, broke out and made for the British Isles, arriving at Rosyth, Scotland, on 14 October, after a dangerous voyage through minefields without charts (which had been confiscated in Estonia) and evading German air and sea patrols.

Operating with the Royal Navy, *Orzel* sank two large enemy troop transports off Norway on 8 April 1940, but failed to return from a patrol in June, and was presumed to have been sunk by a mine. *Sep* was returned to Poland in 1945 and discarded in 1946.

WILK

The *Wilk* (Wolf) and her two sister boats, *Rys* and *Zbik*, were French-built minelaying submarines of the Normand-Fenaux type, ordered in 1926. Basically enlarged versions of the French Saphir class, they were good seaworthy boats but had the major disadvantage of being noisy. Also, their external fuel tanks were prone to leakages and their minelaying system was totally unreliable.

When Germany invaded Poland in September 1939 *Rys* and *Zbik* were both interned in Sweden; they were returned to Poland in 1945 and served for several years in the Polish Navy. *Wilk* was damaged by depth-charges on 2 September 1939, but despite this managed to escape to Britain through the Sund Narrows, reaching Rosyth on 20 September. In June 1940, en route to Norwegian waters, she attacked and sank the Dutch submarine *O13* in error.

She was used as a training boat from September 1940, but because of her poor condition was decommissioned in April 1942. She was towed to Poland in 1951 and later scrapped. Two British U-class submarines, *Urchin* and *P52*, also served under the Polish flag in World War II, as the *Sokol* (Falcon) and *Dzik* (Beast). They gave excellent service in the Mediterranean, where they were known as the "Terrible Twins".

SPECIFICATIONS

WILK

Displacement surfaced: **996tnes (980t)**	Performance surfaced: **14 knots**
Displacement submerged: **1270tnes (1250t)**	Performance submerged: **9 knots**
Machinery: **two screws, diesel/electric motors; 1800/1200hp**	Armament: **six 550mm (21.5in) TT; one 100mm (3.9in) gun; 40 mines**
Length: **78.5m (257ft 6in)**	Surface range: **4632km (2500nm)**
Beam: **5.9m (19ft 4in)**	Crew: **54**
Draught: **4.2m (13ft 9in)**	Launch date: **12 April 1929**

ANGLER

SPECIFICATIONS

ANGLER

Displacement surfaced: **1854tnes (1825t)**	Performance surfaced: **20 knots**
Displacement submerged: **2448tnes (2410t)**	Performance submerged: **10 knots**
Machinery: **twin screws, diesels/electric motors; 5400/2740hp**	Armament: **10 533mm (21in) TT; one 76mm (3in) gun**
Length: **95m (311ft 9in)**	Surface range: **22,236km (12,000nm) at 10 knots**
Beam: **8.3m (27ft 3in)**	Crew: **80**
Draught: **4.6m (15ft 3in)**	Launch date: **4 July 1943**

The US submarine *Angler* was one of the massive Gato class of ocean-going submarines that played havoc with Japan's maritime commerce during the Pacific war, ending with the destruction of the merchant fleet. Under the command of Lt-Cdr Olsen, she opened her score in January 1944, when she sank a small freighter shortly after arriving in her operational area. Another freighter fell victim to *Angler*'s torpedoes in May, while the submarine was operating in the area of the Mandate Islands.

July 1944 found the boat operating off the Philippines and the Malay peninsula under a new skipper, Cdr Hess, who added another ship to the tally, followed by yet another in October.

After the war, together with many other Gato-class boats, *Angler* was rebuilt and given increased engine power and converted to the hunter-killer role. At the end of her operational life in 1963, her propellers were removed, her torpedo tubes welded shut, and she became an immobilized dockside training vessel (*AGSS*), employed to train Naval Reserve personnel. She was used in this role until the 1970s.

The Gato submarines, over 300 of which were built, represented the largest warship construction programme ever undertaken by the United States.

BARB

Another Gato class boat, the USS *Barb* (*SS20*) first operated in Atlantic waters, carrying out a reconnaissance of the Moroccan harbours of Rabat, Fedala, Casablanca, and Safi as well as Dakar in preparation for the Allied landings in North Africa, November 1942.

Transferred to the Pacific, with Lt-Cdr Waterman and Lt-Cdr Fluckey as successive captains, she enjoyed consistent success, and sank six ships in the waters between Formosa and Japan in March and May 1944. In September, *Barb*'s torpedoes claimed two ships totalling 15,906 tonnes (15,655 tons) as well as the 18,085-tonne (17,800-ton) Japanese escort carrier *Unyo*.

The submarine enjoyed further success in November 1944, sinking two ships of 15,505 tonnes (15,261 tons), and January 1945, when the skill of Lt-Cdr Fluckey and his crew sent another five ships to the bottom.

In July 1945, after sinking another enemy vessel with torpedoes, *Barb* made a rocket attack on Japanese positions on Kaihyo Island on the east coast of Karafuto in the Kuriles to the north of Japan; this was the first rocket operation by a submarine.

In 1955, as part of the NATO Mutual Aid Pact, *Barb* was assigned to the Italian Navy and renamed *Enrico Tazzoli*. She was discarded in 1973.

SPECIFICATIONS

BARB

Displacement surfaced:
1854tnes (1825t)

Displacement submerged:
2448tnes (2410t)

Machinery:
twin screws, diesels/electric motors; 5400/2740hp

Length:
95m (311ft 9in)

Beam:
8.3m (27ft 3in)

Draught:
4.6m (15ft 3in)

Performance surfaced:
20 knots

Performance submerged:
10 knots

Armament:
10 533mm (21in) TT; one 76mm (3in) gun

Surface range:
22,236km (12,000nm) at 10 knots

Crew:
80

Launch date:
2 April 1942

CUTLASS

SPECIFICATIONS

CUTLASS

Displacement surfaced: **1570tnes (1860t)**	Performance surfaced: **20 knots**
Displacement submerged: **2467tnes (2420t)**	Performance submerged: **10 knots**
Machinery: **twin screws, diesel/electric motors; 5400/2740hp**	Armament: **10 533mm (21in) torpedo tubes; two 150mm (5.9in) guns**
Length: **93.6m (307ft)**	Surface range: **22,518km (12,152nm) at 10 knots**
Beam: **8.3m (27ft 3in)**	Crew: **85**
Draught: **4.6m (15ft 3in)**	Launch date: **5 November 1944**

Commissioned in March 1945, the USS *Cutlass* belonged to the Tench class of some 50 boats, the last to be laid down in World War II in American yards. They incorporated many lessons learned from the operational use of the Gato-class boats, from which they were developed.

The Tench class were double-hulled ocean-going submarines, more strongly built than the Gatos and with an improved internal layout, which increased the displacement by some 40 tonnes (39 tons). About 20 of the boats were either cancelled or scrapped when partially completed at the point it was realized that Japan could no longer hope to win the war in the Pacific.

For the US Navy's submarine service, the war had begun in a rather downbeat fashion, with torpedoes that constantly failed to detonate and with a serious shortage of submarines, and had ended with the destruction of 1152 Japanese merchant ships of more than 508 tonnes (500 tons), amounting to nearly 5.08 million tonnes (five million tons).

The USS *Cutlass* remained on the US Navy's order of battle until 1973, when she was refurbished and transferred to Taiwan. Another boat, the *Diablo*, went to Pakistan and was sunk by surface forces in the 1971 Indo-Pakistan war.

DACE

One of the later Gato-class boats, USS *Dace* deployed to her operational area in the Pacific in June 1943, under Lt-Cdr McMahon. She sank a Japanese freighter on her first war patrol, but did not register another success until July 1944.

In October 1944, while deployed as part of a submarine group in support of the US landings at Leyte, she sank two ships totalling 13,149 tonnes (12,941 tons) and damaged a third.

A little later, her new commander (now Lt-Cdr Cleggett) brought his boat an even greater success when he attacked and sank the Japanese Takao class cruiser *Maya*.

Under a third skipper, Lt-Cdr Cole, she carried out minelaying operations in December, one enemy merchant ship being sunk as a result.

Dace finished her combat career by sinking a small freighter in Japanese waters in June 1945. After the end of the war she was completely refurbished and modernized, along with many other Gato boats, for delivery to NATO and other friendly navies.

Dace was assigned to the Italian Navy in December 1954 and named *Leonardo da Vinci*. She remained on the active list until well into the 1970s.

SPECIFICATIONS

DACE

Displacement surfaced: **1854tnes (1825t)**	*Performance surfaced:* **20 knots**
Displacement submerged: **2448tnes (2410t)**	*Performance submerged:* **10 knots**
Machinery: **twin screws, diesels/electric motors; 5400/2740hp**	*Armament:* **10 533mm (21in) TT; one 76mm (3in) gun**
Length: **95m (311ft 9in)**	*Surface range:* **22,236km (12,000nm) at 10 knots**
Beam: **8.3m (27ft 3in)**	*Crew:* **80**
Draught: **4.6m (15ft 3in)**	*Launch date:* **25 April 1943**

DRUM

SPECIFICATIONS

DRUM

Displacement surfaced: **1854tnes (1825t)**	**Performance surfaced:** **20 knots**
Displacement submerged: **2448tnes (2410t)**	**Performance submerged:** **10 knots**
Machinery: **twin screws,** **diesels/electric motors;** **5400/2740hp**	**Armament:** **10 533mm (21in) TT;** **one 76mm (3in) gun**
Length: **95m (311ft 9in)**	**Surface range:** **22,236km (12,000nm)** **at 10 knots**
Beam: **8.3m (27ft 3in)**	**Crew:** **80**
Draught: **4.6m (15ft 3in)**	**Launch date:** **15 May 1941**

The USS *Drum* was without doubt one of the most successful American submarines of the Pacific War. On her first deployment, in April 1942, she sank two freighters and the Japanese seaplane carrier *Mizuho* off Japan, and in the following weeks she operated in support of the American defence of Midway Island.

August 1942 found her in the waters off Truk, covering the US landings on Guadalcanal, and between September and October she sank three ships totalling 13,420 tonnes (13,208 tons). In December, her first captain (Lt-Cdr Rice) having handed over to Lt-Cdr McMahon, she torpedoed and damaged the Japanese light carrier *Ryuho.*

After an overhaul, she returned to operational duty in the summer of 1943, sinking another ship in September and one in November. Her torpedoes claimed three more enemy vessels, with another damaged, in October 1944.

During this time there were no fewer than 54 American submarines operating in Japanese waters; by way of contrast, the Japanese could only deploy one boat, the *I-21*, to distant waters, operating between Hawaii and the US west coast.

Drum served until 1962, when she became a reserve training vessel and eventually a museum exhibit.

GATO

Among the first of her class assigned to the US Pacific Fleet, *Gato* departed New London 16 February 1942 for Pearl Harbor via the Panama Canal and San Francisco. On her first war patrol from Pearl Harbor (20 April–10 June 1942), she unsuccessfully attacked a converted aircraft carrier before being driven away by fierce depth-charging off the Marshalls. *Gato*'s first major operational mission was to form part of a submarine screen to the northwest of Midway Island, guarding against a possible Japanese landing. It was to be more than six months before she got her first taste of offensive action, but in January 1943, under Lt-Cdr Foley, she sank four ships totalling 13,205 tonnes (12,997 tons) and damaged four more. She claimed her next victim in November 1943, followed by another in December.

In February 1944, during large-scale offensive air and sea operations around the Caroline Islands, *Gato* sank three more freighters and three small craft while covering the exit channels from the island of Truk. There were further successes in February 1945, when *Gato* (now under Lt-Cdr Farrell) sank a freighter and a corvette.

Gato, along with all the early boats of her class, was laid up at the end of the Pacific war to await disposal in various ways. *Gato*, which was built by the Electric Boat Company, was discarded in 1960.

SPECIFICATIONS

GATO

Displacement surfaced:
1854tnes (1825t)

Displacement submerged:
2448tnes (2410t)

Machinery:
twin screws, diesels/electric motors; 5400/2740hp

Length:
95m (311ft 9in)

Beam:
8.3m (27ft 3in)

Draught:
4.6m (15ft 3in)

Performance surfaced:
20 knots

Performance submerged:
10 knots

Armament:
10 533mm (21in) TT; one 76mm (3in) gun

Surface range:
22,236km (12,000nm) at 10 knots

Crew:
80

Launch date:
21 August 1941

LIZARDFISH

SPECIFICATIONS

LIZARDFISH

Displacement surfaced:
1854tnes (1825t)

Performance surfaced:
20 knots

Displacement submerged:
2448tnes (2410t)

Performance submerged:
10 knots

Machinery:
twin screws,
diesels/electric motors;
5400/2740hp

Armament:
10 533mm (21in) TT;
one 76mm (3in) gun

Length:
95m (311ft 9in)

Surface range:
22,236km (12,000nm)
at 10 knots

Beam:
8.3m (27ft 3in)

Crew:
80

Draught:
4.6m (15ft 3in)

Launch date:
16 July 1944

The USS *Lizardfish* (*SS373*) was one of the last of the Gato-class boats to be built by the Manitowoc shipyard. In July 1945 she deployed to the Southeast Asia theatre, where she and other American submarines operated alongside British boats in mopping up the last Japanese vessels in the area. In the course of these operations, under Cdr Butler, she sank a Japanese submarine chaser. It was during these operations that *Lizardfish*'s sister boat, *Bluefish* (Lt-Cdr Forbes), sank the Japanese seaplane support submarine *I-351*, the only one of her type to be completed.

Late construction boats such as *Lizardfish* were completed with alternative gun mountings fore and aft of the tower, and some were fitted with rocket launchers for shore bombardment (as submarines could approach targets submerged and therefore unseen).

Fully refurbished and improved after World War II, *Lizardfish* remained on the US Navy's active list until January 1962, when she was transferred to the Italian Navy as the *Evangelista Torricelli*.

She was no longer operational by 1970, but was still being used for training and experimental tasks. She was discarded in 1976.

During the 1960s the Italian Navy used nine ex-American ocean-going submarines.

MARLIN

The *Marlin* (*SS205*) and her sister submarine, *Mackerel* (*SS204*) were small, experimental coastal craft built at the request of the US Navy's leading submarine expert, Admiral T.C. Hart, who was conscious of the urgent need to find an effective replacement for the ageing S-type boats and who held the opinion that the ocean-going fleet boats were becoming too large (as in other navies).

Hart's notion that smaller vessels – optimized for the defence of strategic naval bases such as Pearl Harbor and key points like the Panama Canal – should be the subject of a priority building programme, was strongly opposed by other senior US Navy personnel, especially submariners, who knew the importance of deploying large, well-armed, long-range underwater craft that were capable of paralyzing Japan's maritime commerce in distant waters.

Despite the objections, the two boats were built to an Electric Boat Company design; but although they performed well they never saw operational service and were ultimately scrapped. However, six modified boats, fitted with updated equipment, were built for Peru after World War II had ended.

Marlin and *Mackerel* were broken up in 1946 and 1947, respectively.

SPECIFICATIONS

MARLIN

Displacement surfaced: **955tnes (940t)**	Performance surfaced: **16.5 knots**
Displacement submerged: **1158tnes (1140t)`**	Performance submerged: **8 knots**
Machinery: **two screws, diesel engines; 1680hp**	Armament: **six 533mm (21in) TT; one 76mm (3in) gun**
Length: **72.82m (238ft 11in)**	Surface range: **4632km (2500nm)**
Beam: **6.60m (21ft 8in)**	Crew: **80**
Draught: **3.96m (13ft)**	Launch date: **29 January 1941**

NAUTILUS

SPECIFICATIONS

NAUTILUS

Displacement surfaced: **2773tnes (2730t)**	Performance surfaced: **17 knots**
Displacement submerged: **3962tnes (3900t)**	Performance submerged: **8 knots**
Machinery: **twin screws, diesel/electric motors; 5450/2540hp**	Armament: **six 533mm (21in) torpedo tubes, two 152mm (6in) guns**
Length: **113m (370ft)**	Surface range: **18,350km (10,000nm)**
Beam: **10m (33ft 3in)**	Crew: **90**
Draught: **4.8m (15ft 9in)**	Launch date: **15 March 1930**

Formerly designated *V-6*, the USS *Nautilus* and her sister boat, *Narwhal*, were designed as long-range ocean-going cruiser submarines and were virtually identical to the US Navy's sole minelaying submarine, *Argonaut*, except that stern torpedo tubes replaced her minelaying tubes.

In 1940 she was re-fitted as a tanker submarine, the idea being that she would make an ocean or island rendezvous with long-range reconnaissance aircraft (an idea subsequently adopted by the Japanese).

In 1941 both *Nautilus* and *Narwhal* received new engines, and although *Nautilus* was deployed for offensive operations from time to time, her main function throughout the war, mainly because of her long range, was special operations.

In August 1942, for example, both *Nautilus* and *Argonaut* landed a raiding force on Makin, in the Gilbert Islands. In October 1942 she sank two merchant ships in Japanese waters, and in May the following year she and *Narwhal* acted as marker submarines for US marine forces moving in to recapture Attu, in the Aleutian Islands. In March 1944 *Nautilus* sank another large merchant ship off the Mandate Islands. Both *Nautilus* and *Narwhal* were scrapped in 1945.

TANG

One of the few Gato-class boats built by the Mare Island Naval Dockyard, the USS *Tang* had the dubious distinction of going down in history as the submarine that sank herself.

Commanded by Lt-Cdr O'Kane, she began her operational life in February 1944 during Operation Hailstone, the offensive air/sea strikes in the area of the Caroline Islands, when she sank one freighter. During April 1944, operating in support of US carrier forces attacking Japanese-held islands, she rescued 22 shot-down American pilots, sometimes penetrating into the Truk Lagoon to do so under extremely hazardous conditions, a feat that brought Lt-Cdr O'Kane a deserved Medal of Honor.

In June 1944, while operating off Japan, Formosa and the Kuriles, she sank 10 ships totalling 39,787 tonnes (39,159 tons), an impressive result by any standard. She claimed three more Japanese merchant ships in August. In October, operating in the Formosa Strait – an area rich in enemy merchant traffic – she sank another six ships totalling 19,559 tonnes (19,250 tons) in attacks on convoys, as well as torpedoing and damaging two more.

Tang was sunk by one of her own torpedoes, which went out of control and circled her before impacting.

SPECIFICATIONS

TANG

Displacement surfaced: **1854tnes (1825t)**	Performance surfaced: **20 knots**
Displacement submerged: **2448tnes (2410t)**	Performance submerged: **10 knots**
Machinery: **twin screws, diesel/electric motors; 5400/2740hp**	Armament: **10 533mm (21in) TT; one 76mm (3in) gun**
Length: **95m (311ft 9in)**	Surface range: **22,236km (12,000nm) at 10 knots**
Beam: **8.3m (27ft 3in)**	Crew: **80**
Draught: **4.6m (15ft 3in)**	Launch date: **17 August 1943**

TAUTOG

SPECIFICATIONS

TAUTOG

Displacement surfaced: **1498tnes (1475t)**	Performance surfaced: **20 knots**
Displacement submerged: **2408tnes (2370t)**	Performance submerged: **8.7 knots**
Machinery: **twin screws, diesel/electric motors; 5400/2740hp**	Armament: **10 533mm (21in) TT; one 75mm (3in) gun**
Length: **92.2m (302ft 6in)**	Surface range: **20,383km (11,000nm) at 10 knots**
Beam: **8.31 (27ft 3in)**	Crew: **85**
Draught: **4.57 (15ft)**	Launch date: **27 January 1940**

Built by the Electric Boat Company, the Tambor-class submarine USS *Tautog* sank 26 ships during World War II, the biggest toll exacted by any enemy submarine. She was at Pearl Harbor at the time of the Japanese attack on 7 December 1941, but escaped undamaged.

Under Lt-Cdr Willingham, she opened her score in April 1942, sinking two ships in Japanese waters and the submarine *I-28* off Truk, the latter as she was recovering midget submarines.

October 1942, after further successes, found her laying mines off the coast of Indo-China and in the Gulf of Siam, and she opened the new year of 1943 with two more sinkings, her skipper now being Lt-Cdr Sieglaff. In April, she sank another merchantman and the Japanese destroyer *Isonami*.

In January 1944 she repeated her exploit of the previous new year by sinking two more ships, and in March she claimed four more victims, all off Japan. In May 1944, with Lt-Cdr Baskett in command, she sank four more ships, followed by another three in July. Following her new year precedent, she closed her scoreboard by sinking three more transports in January 1945.

Tautog was scrapped in 1960, an ignominious end for a gallant submarine.

TENCH

Although the USS *Tench* had a brief operational career, it was a spectacular one. In May 1945, under the command of Lt-Cdr Baskett – formerly of the USS *Tautog* – she sank six Japanese ships in Japanese waters.

The Tench class boats were improved Gatos, although the external differences were so minor that sometimes no distinction is made between the two. By the time *Tench* became operational in 1945, the Imperial Japanese Navy suffered an almost complete lack of dedicated anti-submarine warfare escort vessels, their destroyers having been expended in fruitless and costly air and surface actions, or torpedoed by submarines.

As a consequence, US submarines were able to run riot in the closing months of the Pacific war, roving at will in Japanese waters. Towards the end of the war, major Japanese surface units were forced to remain penned up in their harbours, where they were subjected to constant air attack.

The majority of the Tench class submarines were cancelled or scrapped incomplete as the war approached its end. At the end of her active life, *Tench* was transferred to the Peruvian Navy in 1976, to be used for spare parts.

SPECIFICATIONS

TENCH

Displacement surfaced: **1570tnes (1860t)**	Performance surfaced: **20 knots**
Displacement submerged: **2467tnes (2420t)**	Performance submerged: **10 knots**
Machinery: **twin screws, diesel/electric motors; 5400/2740hp**	Armament: **10 533mm (21in) torpedo tubes; two 150mm (5.9in) guns**
Length: **93.6m (307ft)**	Surface range: **22,518km (12,152nm) at 10 knots**
Beam: **8.3m (27ft 3in)**	Crew: **85**
Draught: **4.6m (15ft 3in)**	Launch date: **7 July 1944**

D3

SPECIFICATIONS

D3

Displacement surfaced: **948tnes (933t)**	Performance surfaced: **14 knots**
Displacement submerged: **1376tnes (1354t)**	Performance submerged: **9 knots**
Machinery: **twin screws, diesel/electric motors; 2600/1600hp**	Armament: **eight 533mm (21in) TT; one 100mm (3.9in) gun**
Length: **76m (249ft 4in)**	Surface range: **13,897km (7500nm) at 12 knots**
Beam: **6.5m (21ft 4in)**	Crew: **80**
Draught: **3.8m (12ft 6in)**	Launch date: **12 July 1929**

The Russian submarine *D3*, a Series I boat, was serving with the Northern Fleet at the time of Germany's attack on the Soviet Union in June 1941, and deployed to her war station of Norway's North Cape.

On 27 September, commanded by Lt-Cdr F.V. Konstantinov (and with the commander of the 2nd Submarine Division, Capt 2nd Class I.A. Kolyshkin on board) she began a series of attacks on German convoys off the Norwegian coast. All her torpedoes missed their targets. The same thing happened in December, by which time Konstantinov had been replaced Lt-Cdr N.A. Bibeyev.

Bibeyev's aim against the German minelayer *Brummer*, which *D3* attacked on 14 March 1942, was equally as poor, and attacks on German convoys in June 1942 also met with no success. The boat failed to return from a mission in July 1942, presumably sunk by a mine barrage.

The Series I submarines were good seaboats, but their construction was of poor quality and they had a number of design faults. Their diving time, originally, was three minutes, and much work had to be done on the ballast tanks before this was reduced to 30 seconds. Of the six boats in the class, four became war casualties.

D4

Three of Russia's D-class submarines, one of them *D4*, served in the Black Sea during World War II. From May to July 1942, she and all the other submarines assigned to the Black Sea Fleet carried out 77 supply missions to the besieged fortress of Sevastopol, under heavy attack by the Germans. *D4* herself carried out five.

In the summer of 1943, under Lt-Cdr Gremyako, *D4* was assigned to patrol the supply route between Sevastopol, now in German hands, and Constanza in Romania. On 11 August, *D4* sank the 6796-tonne (6689-ton) steamer *Boj Feddersen*, and on 20 August the steamer *Varna*.

Italian midget submarines were active at this time in the hunter-killer role, and on 28 August one of them sank the *Shch 207*. *D4* was sunk on 4 December 1943 by the German sub-chasers *UJ103* and *UJ102* with a barrage of depth-charges.

Of the other two D-class boats deployed in the Black Sea, *D6* was damaged by air attack 96km (60 miles) west of Sevastopol on 18 August 1941; she was subsequently totally destroyed by aerial attack and fire damage while in dry dock at Sevastopol on 12 November 1941.

The third boat, *D5*, performed excellent service and survived the war, being discarded in the 1950s.

SPECIFICATIONS

D4

Displacement surfaced: **948tnes (933t)**	Performance surfaced: **14 knots**
Displacement submerged: **1376tnes (1354t)**	Performance submerged: **9 knots**
Machinery: **twin screws, diesel/electric motors; 2600/1600hp**	Armament: **eight 533mm (21in) TT; one 100mm (3.9in) gun**
Length: **76m (249ft 4in)**	Surface range: **13,897km (7500nm) at 12 knots**
Beam: **6.5m (21ft 4in)**	Crew: **80**
Draught: **3.8m (12ft 6in)**	Launch date: **1929**

K3

SPECIFICATIONS

K3

Displacement surfaced:
  1514tnes (1490t)

Displacement submerged:
  2138tnes (2104t)

Machinery:
  **twin screws,
  diesel/electric motors;
  8400/2400hp**

Length:
  97.65m (320ft 4in)

Beam:
  7.4m (24ft 3in)

Draught:
  4.51m (14ft 10in)

Performance surfaced:
  21 knots

Performance submerged:
  10 knots

Armament:
  **10 533mm (21in) TT;
  two 100mm (3.9in)
  guns; 20 mines**

Surface range:
  **22,236km (12,000nm)
  at 9 knots**

Crew:
  60

Launch date:
  1938

The Series XIV submarine *K3* was one of 12 K-class ocean-going submarines that were developed from several previous proposed designs. The boats were heavily armed, and were intended to carry a small dismantled reconnaissance floatplane known as SPL (*Samolet dlya Podvodnoi Lodki* – aircraft for submarines) which was actually built and test flown, but never entered service.

K3 was in the Baltic at the time of the German invasion, and in August 1941 was transferred to the Northern Fleet via the Stalin (White Sea) Canal, reaching Molotovsk on 25 September. In November, she laid mine barrages off the Norwegian coast, after which she made a number of abortive attacks on German convoys. During one of these, on 26 November, she was attacked by German sub-chasers and depth-charged, being forced to surface. She beat off the German craft in a gun duel, sinking one of them (*UJ1708*). In February 1943, *K3* sank another sub-chaser, together with a large transport.

On 21 March 1943, after making two abortive attacks on enemy convoys, *K3* was attacked by a group of three sub-chasers and sunk. Her commander throughout most of her operational career was Capt 3rd Class Malofeyev.

K21

Like her sister vessel *K3*, *K21* was transferred from the Baltic to the Northern Fleet via Lake Ladoga and the White Sea Canal in August 1941, arriving in September. Her first operational sorties involved laying mine barrages.

In June 1942, operating as part of a force attempting to cover Russian convoys QP.13 and the ill-fated PQ.17, her commander (Captain 2nd Class Lunin) made an unsuccessful attack on the German battleship *Tirpitz*, and in August she attacked a force of German minelayers, again without result.

On 18 February 1943, still under Lunin, she laid a mine barrage off Norway, disembarked some agents and fired six torpedoes into Bogen Bay, where enemy vessels were concentrated, but failed to hit anything. In December of that year, she was deployed against the battlecruiser *Scharnhorst*, which was sunk by the Royal Navy in the Battle of North Cape.

K21 survived the war and remained in service until 1959, when she was decommissioned for use as a permanent training unit at the Polyarnoye naval base. Although the K class boats were among the best available to the Soviet Navy in World War II, they were seldom handled properly and failed to produce the results of which they were capable.

SPECIFICATIONS

K21

Displacement surfaced:
1514tnes (1490t)

Displacement submerged:
2138tnes (2104t)

Machinery:
twin screws,
diesel/electric motors;
8400/2400hp

Length:
97.65m (320ft 4in)

Beam:
7.4m (24ft 3in)

Draught:
4.51m (14ft 10in)

Performance surfaced:
21 knots

Performance submerged:
10 knots

Armament:
10 533mm (21in) TT;
two 100mm (3.9in)
guns; 20 mines

Surface range:
22,236km (12,000nm)
at 9 knots

Crew:
60

Launch date:
1938

L3

SPECIFICATIONS

L3

Displacement surfaced:
1219tnes (1200t)

Displacement submerged:
1574tnes (1550t)

Powerplant:
**twin screws,
diesel/electric motors;
2200/1050hp**

Length:
81m (265ft 9in)

Beam:
7.5m (24ft 7in)

Draught:
7.8m (15ft 9in)

Performance surfaced:
15 knots

Performance submerged:
9 knots

Armament:
**six 533mm (21in)
TT; one 100mm
(3.9in) gun**

Surface range:
9265km (5000nm)

Crew:
54

Launch date:
July 1931

The *L3* was one of six Series II L-class submarines. The boats were modelled on the British submarine *L55*, which had been sunk by Russian destroyers off Kronstadt in June 1919 and later raised.

L3 was in the Baltic at the start of the Russian campaign, and one of her first tasks was minelaying. In August 1942 she was part of a wave of Soviet submarines that broke through the mine barrages laid by German and Finnish naval forces in the Gulf of Finland; these boats began a series of heavy attacks on German supply vessels, *L3* sinking a steamer and probably sinking another. During this period *L3* was commanded by Capt 2nd Class Grischenko.

The onset of winter brought a halt to operations, and when *L3* returned to action minelaying was her main activity. By late 1944 she was once again preying on German transport vessels which, when 1945 began, were mostly involved in evacuating German troops and civilians from East Prussia.

On the night of 16/17 April 1945, *L3* attacked the German steamship *Goya*, which was crowded with refugees. More than 6000 people lost their lives.

L3 survived the war; she was renumbered *B3* in 1945, and was decommissioned and scrapped at Kronstadt between 1959 and 1960.

M172

Originally numbered *M88*, *M172* was a Series XII boat, part of the third batch of M-class small coastal submarines designed to be easily transported by rail in a fully assembled condition.

M172's war operations began with patrols off the Norwegian Polar Coast in July 1941, under the command of Lt-Cdr I.I. Fisanovich, and she opened her score on 12 September 1941 by sinking a small coaster. In May 1942 she came close to being destroyed when she was subjected to an eight-hour depth-charge attack by German submarine chasers, the latter vessels only breaking off when they came under heavy fire from Soviet coastal batteries.

Early in February 1943 *M172* sank a German patrol boat, and during the first months of the year she was involved in a succession of abortive attacks on German convoys along the Polar Coast. Further attacks in September and October 1943 were also conspicuous by their failure, and *M172* failed to return from one such war patrol, possibly lost on one of the flanking mine barrages laid out by the Germans during the summer months. A sister boat, *M174*, was also lost at the same time and in similar circumstances.

Some M-class boats were shipped to the Black Sea in 1944 to harass the German withdrawal.

SPECIFICATIONS

M172

Displacement surfaced: **209tnes (206t)**	Performance surfaced: **14 knots**
Displacement submerged: **221tnes (218t)**	Performance submerged: **8 knots**
Machinery: **single screw, diesel/electric motors; 800/400hp**	Armament: **two 533mm (21in) TT; one 45mm gun**
Length: **44.5m (146ft)**	Surface range: **3484km (1880nm) at 8 knots**
Beam: **3.3m (10ft 10in)**	Crew: **20**
Draught: **3m (9ft 10in)**	Launch date: **1936**

M201

SPECIFICATIONS

M201

Displacement surfaced: **285tnes (281t)**	Performance surfaced: **15.7 knots**
Displacement submerged: **357tnes (351t)**	Performance submerged: **8 knots**
Machinery: **twin screws, diesel/electric motors; 1600/875hp**	Armament: **one 533mm (21in) TT; one 45mm gun**
Length: **49.5m (162ft 5in)**	Surface range: **3484km (1880nm) at 8 knots**
Beam: **4.4m (14ft 5in)**	Crew: **24**
Draught: **2.75m (9ft)**	Launch date: **1940**

The *M201*, a Series XV boat of new design, was under construction at Leningrad when the city came under threat from the advancing Germans in July 1941. The *M201* was evacuated incomplete via Russia's mighty inland waterways to Astrakhan, on the Caspian Sea, for completion.

In April 1943 she set out on the same route, but in reverse, and joined the Northern Fleet in June, beginning patrols off Varangerfjord before the end of the year. Her captain at this time was Lt-Cdr Balin. The latter had bad luck, missing contact with German convoys on two occasions in February 1944 and another one in May.

In June, *M201* joined *S14*, *S104* and *M200* in a combined operation against German convoy traffic off northern Norway. On the 20th, Balin had just got into a good position to attack a convoy when he was sighted by a Heinkel 115 floatplane and forced to dive, being heavily attacked by four German submarine chasers, but she got away. Balin's chance finally came in August 1944, when *M201* closed in and sank the German escort vessel *V6112* off Persfjord, in the light of the midnight sun.

M201 survived the war and was transferred to the Baltic via the White Sea Canal in 1948.

S7

For the crew of the Series IXbis submarine *S7*, operations began on 22 June 1941 with a reconnaissance mission off Gotland. On 26 September, under Capt 3rd Class L.P. Lisin, *S7* sank a small steamer off the Swedish coast. In November, she was involved in special operations, disembarking agents in Narva Bay, Estonia, and on convoy protection duty.

Her first real success on offensive operations came in June and July 1942, when she sank four ships totalling 9311 tonnes (9164 tons); three of these were Swedish, which the Russians regarded as fair game as they were transporting raw materials to Germany.

In September 1942, having broken through enemy mine barrages with a number of other submarines, *S7* was operating in the Aaland Sea, between the Baltic and the Gulf of Bothnia. On 21 October 1942, she was sunk by the Finnish submarine *Vesihiisi* (Lt-Cdr Aittola). Four Russians survived, including Capt Lisin, and were taken prisoner.

The S-class boats to which *S7* belonged were medium-sized submarines designed for open sea warfare, and were built in three progressively improved types. In general appearance, the third series, the Type XVI, resembled the German Type VIIC U-boat.

SPECIFICATIONS

S7

Displacement surfaced: 870tnes (856t)	**Performance surfaced:** 18.75 knots
Displacement submerged: 1107tnes (1090t)	**Performance submerged:** 8.8 knots
Machinery: twin screws, diesel/electric motors; 4000/1100hp	**Armament:** six 533mm (21in) TT; one 100mm (3.9in) gun
Length: 77.5m (255ft 1in)	**Surface range:** 16,677km (9000nm) at 10.5 knots
Beam: 6.4m (21ft)	**Crew:** 46
Draught: 4.06m (13ft 4in)	**Launch date:** 1937

S13

SPECIFICATIONS

S13

Displacement surfaced: **870tnes (856t)**	Performance surfaced: **18.75 knots**
Displacement submerged: **1107tnes (1090t)**	Performance submerged: **8.8 knots**
Machinery: **two screws, diesel/electric motors; 4000/1100hp**	Armament: **six 533mm (21in) TT; one 100mm (3.9in) gun**
Length: **77.5m (255ft 1in)**	Surface range: **16,677km (9000nm) at 10.5 knots**
Beam: **6.4m (21ft)**	Crew: **46**
Draught: **4.06m (13ft 4in)**	Launch date: **1941**

The Type IXbis submarine *S13*'s war began in August 1942 when, commanded by Lt-Cdr Malanchenko, she sank two freighters totalling 3767 tonnes (3704 tons) in the Baltic. On 15 October, operating in Finnish waters, she survived a depth-charge attack by submarine-chasers, but sustained damage that put her out of action for some time.

Her period of real success began in September 1944, when – now under the command of Capt 3rd Class Marinesko – she began offensive operations against German supply and evacuation traffic. On 30 January 1945, when on station 52km (28nm) NNE of Leba, East Prussia, she attacked the 25,893-tonne (25,484-ton) passenger liner *Wilhelm Gustloff*, which was sailing without an escort. The submarine fired a salvo of four torpedoes, three of which found their mark. The liner sank with the loss of some 5200 lives, mostly civilian refugees. Then, on 10 February, still cruising in the same area, *S13* sighted the 14,895-tonne (14,660-ton) passenger ship *General Steuben* and sank her with one hit. Because of the freezing temperature of the water, escort vessels were only able to rescue about 300 of the 3000 persons who had been on board.

S13, the most successful of all Soviet submarines, was decommissioned and scrapped between 1958 and 1959.

S56

The Soviet submarine *S56* had to travel a long way to reach her war station in the Arctic. In October 1942, along with other boats that had been assigned to the Pacific Fleet, she sailed from Petropavlovsk, Kamchatka via Dutch Harbour, San Francisco and the Panama Canal to Halifax, Nova Scotia. From there, *S56*, *S55* and *S54* sailed to Rosyth, Scotland, and then on to the Kola Inlet, which they reached in March 1943.

Her war operations began with patrols off the Norwegian coast in April, and on 17 May, commanded by Capt 3rd Class Shchedrin, she sank the tanker *Eurostadt* and torpedoed a large freighter, but the missile failed to explode.

In July, *S56* sank the minesweeper *M346* and a patrol boat, and in January 1944 she sank the 5080-tonne (5000-ton) freighter *Henrietta Schulte*. In further operations the Soviet boat was not so successful, and on 26 September 1944, while attempting to attack German minesweepers, she was damaged in a depth-charge attack, effectively bringing her wartime career to an end, though not her sailing life.

S56 returned to the Pacific via the Northern Route in the summer of 1950. She was decommissioned in 1959, and became a stationary submarine training unit at the naval base at Vladivostok.

SPECIFICATIONS

S56

Displacement surfaced: **870tnes (856t)**	Performance surfaced: **18.75 knots**
Displacement submerged: **1107tnes (1090t)**	Performance submerged: **8.8 knots**
Machinery: **twin screws, diesel/electric motors; 4000/1100hp**	Armament: **six 533mm (21in) TT; one 100mm (3.9in) gun**
Length: **77.5m (255ft 1in)**	Surface range: **16,677km (9000nm) at 10.5 knots**
Beam: **6.4m (21ft)**	Crew: **46**
Draught: **4.06m (13ft 4in)**	Launch date: **December 1939**

SHCH 307

SPECIFICATIONS

SHCH 307

Displacement surfaced:
595tnes (586t)

Displacement submerged:
713tnes (702t)

Machinery:
**two screws;
diesel/electric motors;
1600/800hp**

Length:
58.5m (191ft 11in)

Beam:
6.2m (20ft 4in)

Draught:
4.3m (14ft 1in)

Performance surfaced:
14 knots

Performance submerged:
8 knots

Armament:
**six 533mm (21in) TT;
two 45mm (1.7in) guns**

Surface range:
**1667km (900nm)
at 8.5 knots**

Crew:
40

Launch date:
1 August 1934

The Shch series of submarines (Shch is an abbreviation of *Shchuka* or Pike) were developed from a 1920s design and were constructed from 1933 until after World War II.

On 28 July 1941, with Lt-Cdr Petrov in charge, *Shch 307* enjoyed an early success when she sank the German submarine *U-144* in the Gulf of Finland. In August, along with other Russian naval units, she was forced to withdraw from Tallin (Estonia) to the main Soviet naval base of Kronstadt as the German armies pushed east, where she remained penned up until September 1942, when she joined the mass breakout into the Baltic through the enemy mine barrages.

In the following weeks, now with Capt 3rd Class Momot in command, *Shch 307* sank one ship and missed three others, and had no further success before she was forced to return to Kronstadt because of ice in November. She fared no better under a new skipper Lt-Cdr Kalinin, when she again broke out in the summer of 1944, missing six targets in rapid succession. Two more misses, in January 1945, brought a less than successful war career to a close.

Shch 307 was scrapped between 1958 and 1959, but her conning tower was preserved at the submarine training school.

SHCH 317

The combat debut of the *Shch 317* occurred in December 1939, during the 'Winter War' with Finland. On 7 December, the Soviet Union declared the Finnish coast from Tornio to Helsinki a blockade zone, later including the Aaland Islands between the Baltic and the Gulf of Bothnia. Five submarines were deployed, including *Shch 317*. One of them (*S1*) sank the German steamer *Bolheim*, and another (*Shch 323*) the Estonian steamer *Kassari*.

In October 1941, *Shch 317* attacked the German light cruiser *Leipzig* in the Baltic, but failed to hit her. However in June 1942, under the command of Lt-Cdr Mokhov, she sank four ships totalling 8416 tonnes (8283 tons) and narrowly missed another.

There was to be no chance of repeating this success. On 12 July 1942, while returning from a war patrol with the Divisional Commander (Capt 3rd Class Egorov) on board, she was attacked repeatedly over a three-day period by German and Finnish submarine-chasers as she passed between two mine barrages. It is not known whether she succumbed to their depth-charges or to the minefields, but she never reached her base. By the beginning of 1943, extensive minefields were making it extremely hazardous for Russian submarines, especially in coastal waters.

SPECIFICATIONS

SHCH 317

Displacement surfaced: 595tnes (586t)	**Performance surfaced:** 14 knots
Displacement submerged: 713tnes (702t)	**Performance submerged:** 8 knots
Machinery: twin screws; diesel/electric motors; 1600/800hp	**Armament:** six 533mm (21in) TT; two 45mm (1.7in) guns
Length: 58.5m (191ft 11in)	**Surface range:** 1667km (900nm) at 8.5 knots
Beam: 6.2m (20ft 4in)	**Crew:** 40
Draught: 4.3m (14ft 1in)	**Launch date:** 25 September 1935

INDEX